Acknowledgments

As I reflect on the writing of this book, I find there are many people whose imprint is in some way ingrained on the fabric of these pages. Herb Hill, my father, role model, and mentor; Natalie Hill, my mother, whose untimely death prevented her from experiencing the love of my daughter; Robert F. Hostage, whose publishing decision made this book possible; Hilary Swinson, my editor, for her high level of professionalism; and my aunt Thelma Schilber for her lifetime love. I also wish to acknowledge the many generous people who have given me support and encouragement, including but not limited to Michael and Janice Woods, Fred and Phyllis Allen, Rodney Marble, and all the divorced parents who shared their experiences with me.

DIVORCED FATHER

*Coping with Problems
Creating Solutions*

Gerald A. Hill, Ph.D.

BETTERWAY PUBLICATIONS, INC.
WHITE HALL, VIRGINIA

Published by Betterway Publications, Inc.
P.O. Box 219
Crozet, VA 22932
(804) 823-5661

Cover design by Susan Riley

Library of Congress Cataloging-in-Publication Data

Hill, Gerald A.
    Divorced father.

    Includes index.
    1. Divorced fathers--United States.
2. Single-parent family--United States.
3. Parenting--United States.   4. Custody
of children--United States.   I. Title.
HQ756.H55   1989   306.8'9   88-34969
ISBN: 1-55870-113-3

Printed in the United States of America
0 9 8 7 6 5 4 3 2

For my daughter Taryn, who is a radiant gift for the future.

For my wife Rosalyn, whose enlightenment and support are an inspiration.

And with deep appreciation to Mary Nealon, who is truly a saint.

Contents

Introduction.. **9**

1 Getting Through . . . Just After the Divorce.........**13**

2 Your Self-Image **23**

3 The Case for a Parenting Partnership **31**

4 Child Custody and Visitation **39**

5 Finding the Right Lawyer **71**

6 Making a Home for Yourself and Your Child...... **83**

7 Your Parenting Style... **95**

8 Communication.. **99**

9 Family Activities... **113**

10 Discipline **121**

11 Your Child's Chores and Allowance **127**

12 Stamping Out Manipulation **131**

13 Finding the Right Babysitter............................. **137**

14 You, Your Child, and the School......................... **141**

15 The Miracle of Love: Dating and Remarriage .. **153**

16 The Gift of Child-Centered Time....................... **169**

17 A Letter to My Daughter..................................... **175**

Suggested Reading and Reference **181**

Action Organizations... **183**

Endnotes.. **185**

Index... **187**

Introduction

My wife moved out of our home just a month before our daughter Taryn was born. That was six years ago. After the shock of the divorce had waned, I pulled myself together like an earthquake survivor and surveyed the ruins, my daughter's future my most pressing concern. I saw her twice a week, but it was never enough. Half of each visit was awkwardly consumed in reestablishing the closeness our previous visit had ended with. I felt angry, betrayed, and bereaved.

I set about figuring out how, once and for all, to establish a real father-daughter bond, so I could be a major and continuous influence in Taryn's life. The result was a war-like plan that locked me into a life-and-death battle with my former spouse. And I was determined to win.

A physical fitness program to clear my mind for battle was part of my plan. Mornings, I jogged with Fred Allen, a friend of many years, through the San Francisco suburb where I had taken an apartment. Fog-chilled air rolled in off the gray ocean, the astringent scent of eucalyptus poured down from towering trees.

My senses sharpened and my mind began to clear. Fred's companionship banished my sense of alienation, and I was beginning to establish a more continuous closeness to my daughter. Everything was looking a little brighter.

One particular day, when our schedules conflicted, I jogged alone late in the evening. Not far from my apartment, I saw my former spouse's car parked in the silver disk of light under a street lamp. Her back toward me, she was making a telephone call at an outdoor booth. In her car a young man held a little girl, his right arm around her, his face tilted down, smiling, talking. The child, her eyes shining in the light of the street lamp, gazed trustingly into his face, her own rapt with attention. Her light brown hair, sparkling in the lamp light, seemed close enough to touch, and my hand ached to reach out and touch it. The little girl was my daughter.

To a stranger, the group under the street lamp would have appeared to be a family. To me, it was a death sentence.

Panic overwhelmed me: I had been pushed out of my daughter's life, my place taken by this man who held her so comfortably in his arms, who had usurped my place in her heart. Shock froze me to the spot. Suddenly I was as cold as if I had been physically cast into a refrigerated truck. My knees weakened and wavered, like those of an invalid standing for the first time after a long illness. My heart pounded, but my hands felt numb, completely drained of blood. Disoriented, I was stranded somewhere back in those bleak days when I had lost hope of building a father-daughter relationship with my child. With the same fierce intensity with which I would have rescued her from a kidnapper, I wanted to take my child back from that man. But I could not move. Shortly, my former spouse returned to the car, got in, and drove away, while I stood encased in a block of ice. I had heard people talk about being frozen in their tracks by shock, but I never really believed it. Now I do.

The short walk back to my apartment was the most important and the most painful journey of my life. With pain came insight. I had wanted a miracle, so I had instructed my mind to make the miracle come true. My mind devised a logical Win-Lose plan, the very nature of which required a loser; without a loser there could be no winner. Win-Lose thinking identifies the enemy and the winner must defeat that enemy.

But the heart knows no enemies. My plan, flawed by the limitations of pure rationalism, had failed because neither the mind nor the heart alone can create a miracle; it takes both mind and heart. Together they point the way to Win-Win-Win triangles, in which there is no enemy, no one to defeat. Everyone — my daughter, my former spouse, and I — all could win. If I seriously wanted a real miracle, it was time to scrap my Win-Lose plan and get to work on a WinWin-Win plan.

I have heard people talk about miracles they experienced, but I never really believed them. Now I do. This was my first miracle, the first of many that happened to me and that can happen to you.

The material and the motivation for this book spring from the personal pain and bewilderment of being a divorced father, and from research for my doctoral dissertation, but mainly from the miracles that my Win-Win-Win plan has created in my life. I have found some constructive solutions to the problems of divorced fathers. I hope you will find them useful, and that they will bring you the happiness and peace they have given me.

Don't believe it when people tell you that you have to learn the hard way, from painful personal experience. That's just an old-fashioned idea. You can, and I hope you will, learn from others' experience, including mine.

I hope that, years from now, you won't have to say — as I have said many times — "If I only knew then what I know now." Let me tell you what I know now that I didn't know then. Let me help clear the path for you.

One further note, if I may, before we proceed on our quest of miracles.

We are all somewhat dimly aware of the technicalities of formal English that demand the agreement of nouns and verbs, and end up in thought-out constructions like, "When you speak to your child, you must tell him or her. . ." Language requirements are further compounded by anti-discrimination rules requiring equal time for boys and girls. Some authors resolve this problem by alternating the sex of the child in succeeding chapters. Chapter 1 speaks of a boy, Chapter 2 speaks of a girl, Chapter 3 reverts to a boy, and so on throughout the book. I'm impressed by the ingenuity of this solution, but I find my attention focusing on the author's skill rather than on his (or her) message. I respect scholarly precision in its place; but its place is not in this book.

I am the father of one child, Taryn, whom I deeply love. I suffered wrenching pain by being separated from her when she was very young. It is six years later. I have remarried. My wife and I have established a new home. I have come out whole, happy, and an important part of Taryn's life. I know you can do the same thing, and I would like to dispense with any technicalities that get in the way of straight talk.

I want to talk to you about my experience, and I think more clearly when I think in terms of my own child. I hope that, whether you have a daughter, or a son, or several of each, you will understand that, when I speak of one child, and whether I refer to "her" or "him," I speak of any child and of all children. I want to talk with you as honestly and clearly as though we were sitting across a table from each other, having a quiet cup of coffee, and talking about our children.

I cannot think of any need in childhood as strong as the need for a father's protection.

— Sigmund Freud

Chapter 1

Getting Through . . . Just After the Divorce

*The man who cannot survive bad times
will not see good times.*

— Hasidic saying

This is the time when you must recover from the shock of divorce; reach out to the people who can help you, to get your priorities in line, eat sensibly, sleep well, exercise, and plan to perform miracles.

But first, be sure your child is surrounded with all the love and protection she needs during this transitional period.

YOUR CHILD'S WELFARE — YOUR FIRST PRIORITY

Supervision

Your child's welfare remains your responsibility and your right, whether she lives with you, your former spouse, or others. Make sure that her primary caretaker is mentally, physically, and financially able to provide the care, guidance, and support she needs to survive the transitional period unscathed.

Know who her friends are. Don't take secondhand information. Check it out yourself.

Love

Your love is important to your child's proper development. She needs assurance that you love her, and the best way to assure her is to tell her. Especially during this sensitive period, when she is struggling with her own insecurities and may feel she caused all the trouble that's going on around her, tell her you love her, and tell her often.

Security

Help her understand that you will never desert her, that you will always be there, that she will always be loved and cared for. Talk to her about the future, and encourage her to tell you what she thinks it will be like. Ease her fears. Form your own mental picture of the future, what her needs will be, and how they will be met. Then convey this picture to her in clear and simple terms. Let your words and your voice tell her how safe and wonderful and exciting the future will be.

Communication

Communicate with her — fully and frequently. Always be honest and open. Resist the temptation to give a "child's answer," if what you mean by that is an evasion of the truth on the self-serving premise that it's not important because a child doesn't know the difference. There is no such thing as a "child's answer," it's only a euphemism for "lie." There are two kinds of truth: accurate facts phrased for the understanding of an adult and accurate facts phrased for the understanding of a child. There are two kinds of lies: the "child's answer," and the good old-fashioned falsehood.

In these troubled and rapidly changing times, you can be an invaluable guide to your child, and the older she gets the more valuable you will be. But it is not enough that a guide knows and tells the truth; it is necessary that the person being guided believes the guide to be trustworthy. This applies equally to the wilderness of life as it does to the wilderness of nature.

Right now is the only time you can establish the foundation for open and honest communication. Some things can be put on hold until everything settles down. This is not one of them. Don't learn to your regret that children, even very young children, understand more than you think. If she catches you twisting or evading, your credibility flies right out the window, and with it go your credentials as a trustworthy guide.

YOUR OWN WELFARE — YOUR SECOND PRIORITY

You are not alone with your problems. There are people who can, and will, help you. Keep looking for them and you'll find them. In the meantime, you'll run across people who do not understand what you're going through. Don't judge them too harshly; you and I may not have been very sympathetic until we'd gone through hell ourselves.

After a divorce, friends are sympathetic. They take your hand, look deeply into your eyes and, in the hushed tone used to address the family of the recently departed, say, "I'm so sorry to hear about it." Then the helpful type claps you on the arm and adds, "Take care of yourself." But they never say what "IT" means. They don't have to; we know that "IT" is a conventional substitute for anything we want to avoid naming. They don't say, "I'm sorry to hear your grandfather died," or "I'm sorry to hear you got fired," or "I'm sorry to hear about your divorce." They say they are sorry to hear about "IT."

This convention doesn't create confusion because we rarely endure two concurrent losses sufficiently unpleasant to warrant the use of "IT." But "IT" signals that the sympathy will fade. It's like when you call in sick. The boss automatically responds: "I'm sorry to hear it. Take care of yourself." But the sympathy shortly turns into polite inquiries about how soon you can get back to work. That doesn't prove that the boss's heart is hard. All of us soon lose sympathy with pains we can't feel. That's the way life is.

Your friends can't feel your pain, they can't see it. They think they have given you enough time, and they begin to inquire, somewhat impatiently, when you're going to be your old self again. They act as though you've had a bad cold and they have given you enough time to get over it — and there you go coughing again.

It's like when the boss calls to ask how you are and when you're coming back. Of course, work is piling up. You want to get back to the job; nobody wants to be sick. But you know you have to take care of yourself and get better before you can work. Yet, illogically, you feel guilty because you are not working.

And now life is piling up. You want to get back to living; nobody wants to be in pain, out of step with his friends, a stranger in his own world. But your trauma is real, and you need time to get past it before you can be your old self again.

Despite that, sometimes you feel guilty and you begin to wonder if your pain is all in your mind or if it's real.

Your trauma is indeed real — as real as a broken arm, as painful as a bad tooth. Don't try to go through it all alone. Get help.

FIND THE PEOPLE WHO CAN AND WILL HELP YOU, AND ACCEPT THEIR HELP

As you grope your way through this difficult period, people will divide into two groups: those who don't understand what you are going through and those who do. Don't waste your time feeling bitter about the first group. They are not callous. They just don't understand your grief. Accept the fact that they live in a different world, the kind you lived in before shock destroyed your happiness and taught you the meaning of grief. Find the support you need in the second group, which breaks down into three broad categories:

1) People who understand and want to help you because they love you unconditionally. They love you because you are you. They feel your pain and feel your happiness; your happiness makes them happy, and your sadness makes them sad. The strength of their love gives them an intuitive, emotional understanding of your grief and a desire to help you through it. You most frequently find these people in your immediate family or among long-time friends. But you find them elsewhere, too . . . a neighbor, someone you work with, an old school friend. Find them and accept their help.

2) Self-help groups who understand and want to help you because they have experienced the same heartbreak. These people are suffering through, or have suffered through, the same overwhelming loss you now endure. They will not fix time limits on your recovery; they know it takes as long as it takes. They will help you survive. They will share your pain, relieve your isolation, give you a sense of being among friends, a member of a warm and welcoming community. These groups, composed of fathers without custody of their children, are springing up everywhere in response to the increasing number of fathers reaching out for help. The groups and their names differ from region to region, but you can locate them quickly through community health organizations, churches, and hospitals. Find them and accept their help.

3) Professionals who understand and who want to help you because that is the purpose for which they have been trained and to which they have devoted their lives. They can get you back on the right path if your life gets out of control despite the best efforts of those around you.

Crisis symptoms take many forms. Watch for them: inability to do your job; overwork, excessive anger, fatigue, headaches, insomnia, nightmares, loneliness, guilt, fear, disorientation, and self-pity; excessive use of alcohol or drugs; wild mood swings, depression, or any drastic departure from your usual way of thinking or acting.

If any of these danger signals appear, consult a psychiatrist, psychologist, psychiatric social worker, clergyman with specialized training, or other licensed mental health worker, or join a counseling group. To find the kind of assistance that will give you the best support, check with a mental health association, local hospital, community health organization, or your personal physician. These resources can tell you how to locate the right person, and just one or two consultations can sometimes make a world of difference. If you need their assistance, find them and accept their help.

YOUR TRAUMA IS REAL, STRESSFUL, AND DANGEROUS

A recent study documents the stressful nature of the period immediately following divorce. Men recently divorced are nine times more likely to wind up in a psychiatric hospital than men from intact families. (Under similar circumstances, women are only three times more likely to require psychiatric hospitalization than women from intact families.) [1] Another study indicates that deaths from heart disease, cancer, automobile accidents, homicides, and suicides also increase. [2]

Stress can disable and even kill. Take it seriously.

Even the popular press warns of its danger and rightly so. We have all seen the Do-It-Yourself Stress Tests in magazines and newspapers. They list major life events, assign points to each event indicating the amount of stress it creates, and provide instructions for taking and rating the test. Most of us have pulled out a pencil, checked the events in our lives, totalled the number of stress points, and consulted the index to find out how we stand.

Those of us who checked off "marital breakup" or "loss of a child or loved one" know that these life events rank right up there at the top with "death in the family." Tests may differ a few points one way or another, but they all place us at the high-risk end of the spectrum; they all warn us: "Take Care."

COMMONSENSE "TAKE CARE" RULES THAT WORKED FOR ME

RULE #1: Avoid accidents.

After a divorce or unfavorable custody decision expect accidents. You will spill your coffee, trip over the rug, slam the door on your fingers, or find yourself crossing against a red light, and wonder why. Grandma could have warned you. "Land sakes, Sonny," she would have said, "Look where you're going, and keep your mind on what you're doing." She was right. Your stressed mind attaches itself to you like a balloon attaches itself to a little kid. The balloon drifts with each passing breeze and, without a firm hand, it darts away forever in the first strong wind. Your mind, under stress, overreacts to every random thought. It flinches aside to avoid a painful memory, dashes back to slam a door against guilt, and surges forward reaching for an idyllic tomorrow. Absorbed in its own concerns, it ignores its responsibility to supervise your body, and your body, a well-programmed but unthinking computer, carries you straight to the nearest available accident.

Call your mind down from the attic. Don't let it sit up there rummaging through yesterday's memories and daydreaming about a perfect tomorrow while your body goes stumbling into trouble. Keep telling your mind about the work that's to be done here and now. Talk to it. (Silently, please. Don't add to your problems by unnecessarily acquiring a reputation for eccentricity.) Point out problems: "Hey there, don't trip over the rug." "Watch the traffic, Buddy! It's a red light." Tell it what your eyes see: "My car needs washing." "The sun looks happy today." Tell it what your ears hear: "That's the alarm clock. Time to get up." "How can those sea gulls sound so raucous and look so graceful?" Keep nudging your mind to take care of business, and remember Grandma: "Look where you're going, and keep your mind on what you're doing." You'll be a lot safer.

RULE #2: Keep your priorities in line.

Stress can blast your sense of priorities. Trivial details acquire monumental urgency. You stop on the way to answering the phone in order to balance your checkbook, which you interrupt to polish your shoes, which you leave unfinished to alphabetize the books on the bookshelf. The next morning, you wonder why you get out of bed feeling exhausted, disorganized, pressured, and threatened by dark clouds of things undone and things that skipped your mind.

It's time to start making lists. Take a big sheet of lined paper. At the top, write: URGENT: Business. At random, and as quickly as you can, jot down everything you must do at work. If you write down anything that's not really important, cross it off. Don't waste time making this first list neat. It doesn't matter how sloppy it looks, it's just a draft. Then look over the list, and decide which is most urgent, which you should take care of first. Place a "1" in front of it. Decide which is next most important, place a "2" in front of it, and continue numbering the items according to their importance until you have numbered them all.

Now you are ready to make your real list. On a clean sheet of lined paper, enter the heading: URGENT: Business. Then, starting with #1, list all the items in numerical order, one to a line. When you finish this, take another sheet of lined paper. Head it URGENT: Personal. List your personal tasks in exactly the same way. Now you have right in front of you a two-page game plan containing everything that's important: clearly stated, organized, ready for action. Keep these lists handy, and as you finish a job, cross it off and congratulate yourself on achieving an important step. I enjoy slashing jobs from the list, in fact, sometimes the anticipation motivates me to do unpleasant jobs.

Every night, just before you go to sleep, check to see that all finished jobs are deleted, and slowly read over the remaining lists. It's important to do this just before you sleep. When you are tired (as when you are hypnotized), it's easier to access your unconscious. During the night, your unconscious mind will mull over the next day's jobs and, with luck, you will wake next morning with a great new idea, a miraculous solution to your problem. Put your unconscious mind to work every night, and you'll get used to jumping out of bed in the morning feeling like a million dollars with fresh, new solutions popping into your conscious mind.

RULE #3: Slow down.

Stress can throw you into overdrive. Your adrenal glands kick into heavy production. Adrenalin pounds through your body, your tempo zooms; you think you can, and you think you must, do everything at the same time. You feel great for the moment. Bursts of frenetic activity, no matter how pointless, fill your mind and protect you from unpleasant thoughts. They create a sense that you're accomplishing important tasks and fill you with a specious euphoria that says everything's going to be just fine. In hindsight, your energy exhausted, you know you've been kidding yourself, making a mess of things, and now you have to patch up your mistakes. You would be further ahead if you had taken your time and done it right.

Rushing about mindlessly is addictive because it provides an escape from reality. At the same time, it reinforces itself by creating the pleasurable illusion that you are moving quickly in the right direction. It is not always easily overcome. It is time for further silent conferences with your mind.

Hold your mind to the standards of the fire engine driver. Judicious speed is commendable on the way to a fire; speeding back from the fire just for the rush it gives you is irresponsible. Make it clear to your mind that you expect it to maintain a steady, responsible pace; that it is permitted to race your body only in a valid emergency. Always question speed. If you find yourself pushing, stop and ask "Why? Do I have to finish this project immediately?" "Why? What's going to happen if I don't?" "Do I have to meet a specific deadline? Can I ease up and still make the deadline?"

Slow down. Deliberately sit back and relax. Turn on the music, look out the window, move around for a few minutes. Then return and pick up the project at a calmer pace. You'll make fewer mistakes, get more done, and feel a lot better.

RULE #4: Drive as though you are taking a driver's license test.

The moment your car moves into third gear, your mind will try to wander off and think its own thoughts. Sooner or later, it will dredge up an infuriating memory that hits you like a dentist's drill hitting a nerve. Your anger will explode, your foot will reflexively stomp the gas and, if it's your lucky day, you'll get a ticket. That'll wake you up. Snap you right back to present-time consciousness, it will. On the other hand, you could slaughter an innocent human being. You won't know real agony until you try living with the knowledge that you have ruined someone else's life.

Every time we take the wheel, we literally take other lives in our hands. We know this. But driving becomes so automatic we lose sight of its awesome responsibility. Keep your mind on what you're doing; don't let it drift off. A simple solution: every time you step into your car, tell yourself you are taking a driver's license test. Picture the driving inspector sitting in the passenger's seat. Be aware of the critical eye, the stern, silent mouth, the disapproving expression, and drive by the book.

Everyday caution is far more important than any driver's test you will ever take. Keep your car in A-1 condition. Know exactly where you are going, and be prepared to think fast. Snap on the seat belt. Watch for children, pedestrians, bicycles, emergency vehicles, road and weather hazards. Don't speed. Don't tailgate. Don't make unnecessary lane changes. Start early, drive patiently, and don't take your anger out on other drivers.

RULE #5: Take care of your physical health.

"He who has health has hope, and he who has hope has happiness." That's just as true today as it was 2,000 years ago when Plutarch wrote it. It is especially true during a depression that follows separation from your child. Ties to the past and the future are disrupted, goals can become pointless, effort can become futile. Life itself loses its value, and your health takes a low priority. You become careless and inattentive, and your mental and physical health deteriorate just at the time when you need them most. Don't let this happen. You need all the health and hope you can summon.

If you run into any serious health problems, consult a professional. Otherwise, just follow simple time-tested health maintenance rules.

Nutrition

If you must drink, do it moderately. Very moderately. Drinking excessively to forget your problems is like eating fudge to forget you're gaining weight. Limit alcohol, coffee, fats, rich desserts, and fast foods.

Eat regularly and sensibly. Select food the same way you select gas for your car — with an eye to optimum performance. Eat a broad range of foods, low in calorie, high in the proteins, carbohydrates, vitamins, and minerals you need for top mental and physical performance. A healthy diet doesn't require a lot of fussing or measuring and weighing of food. You'll find some basic food and snack suggestions in Chapter 9.

Sleep

With all the adjustments and tensions you are enduring, you have to expect some insomnia. But you can decrease it.

Insomnia tortured me until I discovered I was creating most of it myself. I let my mind go round and round all day replaying distressing memories like a needle on a record, until it dug such deep grooves I couldn't stop it at night. Experience taught me two successful coping techniques I'd like to pass along to you. Painful memories kept me awake. That was my main problem, but I solved it. Immediately after a painful incident, I would deliberately think about something funny or happy or hopeful, and I would keep thinking about it until I forgot the incident. This stopped my mind from making a permanent record. But it works only if you do it immediately; once the memory gets a foothold, it forms a memory groove, and once it does that it will haunt you day and night.

Another problem: In the middle of the night, I would wake abruptly, in darkness and silence, without sight or sound of human presence, disoriented and uncertain whether I was surrounded by reality or an evil dream; it was eerie, dreary, and depressing. But I learned to outwit it by playing a radio, very low, all night long. The talk shows helped most; they diverted my mind from my problems and helped me go to sleep. I continued to wake in the night, but it was less abrupt and less unpleasant. I seemed to drift up from deep sleep, through several levels of increasing consciousness. I was aware that I was waking and that I was listening to a talk show, and voices and ideas humanized the darkness as I regained full consciousness.

Exercise

For sparkle, energy, confidence, and optimism; for the ability to work harder and think more clearly — try exercise. Regular vigorous exercise, at least twenty to thirty minute periods three to four times a week, strengthens the heart and cardiovascular system, and lowers stress, blood pressure, and cholesterol. By stimulating norepinephrine it activates brown-fat metabolism, and helps control your weight; by stimulating the release of endorphins and enkephalins, nature's natural uppers, it gives you a natural high, similar in character but lower in intensity, to the "Runner's High."

If health problems restrict your activity, consult your doctor before you undertake a strenuous program. Otherwise, there's no time like today to start and there's no limit to the possibilities: aerobics, baseball, basketball, body building, calisthenics, hiking, jogging, skating, skiing, soccer, swimming, tennis, walking, wrestling. That you exercise is important; how you exercise is not important. So find something that gives you pleasure. You'll stick with it a lot longer and, in addition to the obvious and measurable physical benefits, you will derive a wonderful sense of enjoyment, well being, and self-confidence.

Chapter 2

Your Self-Image

*The prisoner who had lost faith in the future — his future
— was doomed. With his loss of belief in the future, he
also lost his spiritual hold; he let himself decline and became subject to mental and physical decay.*

— Viktor E. Frankl, *Man's Search For Meaning*, discussing how
prisoners survived the World War II concentration camps. [1]

These words apply, with equal force, to the personal hell of despair
the divorced father must survive if he hopes to create miracles in his
child's life. Keep a firm day-to-day spiritual hold on your faith in tomorrow. Believe in yourself. Believe in the future. Believe you will
make miracles happen, and the future will prove you right.

ENJOY AND RESPECT YOUR FREEDOM

Immediately after the divorce, most of us begin to rewrite the past,
exaggerating its happiness and editing out its pain. I was no exception, until one day a business associate exposed my romanticized version of yesterday as a self-deception that only increased my pain. I
pass his sagacious advice on to you: "Jerry, you're only making yourself miserable," he said. "Don't sentimentalize yesterday. By remem-
bering it as better than it was, you make today, by contrast, worse
than it is. Do yourself a favor — reverse that mind game you're
playing, and concentrate on today. You'll be a lot happier."

His advice worked I discovered, as I trained my mind on today,
starting with small things like the garbage. "I don't," I told myself,
"have to take the garbage out right now. I don't have to take it out
tomorrow. In fact, I don't ever have to take it out if I don't want to."
Then I said to the garbage, "You there, you just sit there until I feel
like taking you out." And it did.

As I extended the theory to larger areas of my life and became
more aware of my freedom, I found that for the first and probably the
last time in my life, I was free to act without consulting anyone, free

to do exactly as I wished, and I began to use my time more constructively and to accept full responsibility for creating my own happiness. Was I lonesome? Yes, very. Was I selfish in enjoying my freedom? No, I was positive, appreciating what this day gave me, instead of crying about what it took away.

Enjoy the freedom and luxury of flexible hours. In the future you may well find yourself accommodating your time to the preferences of others. Right now, other than your work hours, your time's your own. Use it well, and enjoy it.

Let moderation be your guide in everything — especially in personal relationships. The wreckage of your marriage can temporarily impair your judgment and damage your self-image, driving you, like a shipwrecked sailor, to clutch desperately at any kind soul who can help you get your feet back on the ground. It's easy, under these circumstances, to mistake gratitude for love.

Avoid impulsive entanglements. Keep romance on a friendly basis, and guard against making (or believing) wild, unrealistic commitments which, in a saner light, can embarrass you and hurt some really nice people.

BURNISH YOUR SELF-IMAGE

The most unpleasant thing about marriage is that it's the only time in your adult life when you have to stand still and listen to what's wrong with you. You can tell your friends to shut up; you can split on a partner; you can walk out on an employer. But a spouse you've got to listen to, and constant complaints, whether they are valid or merely venomous, can tarnish your self-image.

Your self-image is your total conception of yourself and your identity, including your good points and your bad points, your strengths and your weaknesses. It tells you who you are, what you are, what you can do, what you can't do, and what other people think about you and, despite the fact that it lies a lot, you trust its opinions. Current psychological research shows that many people are poor judges of what other people think about them. Shy people who think others dislike them are frequently considered quite likeable, and many sociable people who think they bring joy into the lives of others are frequently considered objectionable.

Your self-image, like Topsy in *Uncle Tom's Cabin*, just grew. Behavorial scientists generally agree that it is similar to a mosaic, bits and pieces collected from here and there, voices from the past hoarded in your mind until they form your own picture of yourself. Sociologist Charles Cooley's "Looking Glass" theory maintains that a child forms his self-picture by observing how people (parents, siblings, peers, teachers) respond to him. He looks at others as though they are mirrors in which he can discover his own identity. If the human mirror reflects him as lovable, he sees himself as lovable and incorporates the quality in the self-portrait in his head. If instead, people reject him, he feels worthless and adds that quality to his portrait. Anthropologist Margaret Mead, in an analogous theory, contends that the child, by looking at himself through the eyes of grownups, discovers that he, although smaller, is also a human being, and adds humanness to his self-picture. Psychologist Eric Berne's *Games People Play* broadens the general public's understanding of how a critical parental voice can adversely influence a person's opinion of himself and his abilities throughout his life.

Your self-image can point you toward success or turn you away from it. For instance, if you see yourself as a winner, you will ask for a raise confidently and probably get it, but if you see yourself as a loser, you won't even get up the courage to ask. Or say you're speaking at a company meeting. If you see yourself as an interesting speaker, you'll probably knock them dead, but if you see yourself as inept you'll be just that. You'll bumble around and make a mess of it.

YOU DON'T HAVE TO BE A VICTIM

Psychologist Wayne W. Dyer, a widely read and highly respected author, points out the need to work at building a healthy self-image.". . . Your own self-image can contribute to your being victimized in life. If you believe that you can't do something, that you're unattractive, that you're not intelligent . . . you will also believe that others see you that way, and you will act that way, and even be that way. Working at healthy self-images is crucial if you are to avoid being a knee-jerk victim, with responses as predictable as when the doctor smacks your knee with a little hammer . . . "[2]

If you use your imagination, you will find innumerable ways to victimize yourself. But by applying your imagination in constructive ways, you can, by the same token, find the means to eliminate your victim status. The choice is yours.

CHANGING YOUR SELF-IMAGE

To change your self-image, you have first to overcome inertia and break deeply rooted habits. If you prefer the familiar, however painful, like the prisoner who returns to prison because he can't cope with change; if you cling to old habits and old ways, however destructive, you may find it difficult to change your self-image. If, on the other hand, you have the courage to risk change and the strength to accept responsibility for your own actions, you will find image-changing a rewarding adventure.

Second, you must assert your right to control your own thinking. Negative voices pollute your mental atmosphere just as chemicals pollute your physical atmosphere. Take a stand against self-invited voices that invade your thoughts, diminish your capabilities, and demean your character. They have no more right to hang out in your head than uninvited guests have to hang out in your home.

And third, the decisive step: evict the voices from your mind.

The Eviction Process

1. Make the decision. Nothing will happen until you do.

2. Find a quiet place where you will be undisturbed. Calmly summon the internal voices, one by one, and listen to each elucidate your faults. Jot the faults down; it will pull them outside your mind and put them on the table where you can study them more objectively.

3. Evaluate the faults carefully, and throw away all the junk complaints. Picture yourself standing on the verge of a volcano, throwing them into its glowing maw. Watch them curl into blackened wisps of burned paper tossed high in the roaring forces of molten rock and falling back into the crater's rage, destroyed and gone forever.

4. I specified "junk complaints" because, just possibly, you may snatch something useful from the garbage heap. If a hunter keeps shooting at the sky he will, sooner or later, bring down a duck and, if your former wife complained enough, she probably hit on a truth here and there. Don't throw these away; they can be valuable. If a criticism is valid, own up to it and correct it. What could be more ironic than to make use of a complaint that was intended to hurt you in order to make yourself over and become more attractive to other people.

5. Don't be a complaint collector. Once you've tossed out all the rubbish and your mind is cleared, stuff it to the brim with positive images about yourself. Then guard the entrance. Admit nothing but constructive ideas, great memories, and friendly pictures. Don't let anyone use your head as a dumping ground.

6. Think about yourself objectively, as though you were another person. Look at that other person and make a list of the things about him you like and respect: his appearance, his personality, his consideration for others, his sense of humor, his intelligence, and his skills. Don't overlook his less cosmic but more personalized virtues: his ability to make a great omelette, his knowledge of comic books, or wine,

or classic cars. List, in other words, all of the things that impress you when you observe them in others, but which, although you may be aware of possessing them yourself, never seem to add to your stature in your own eyes. Train yourself to admire yourself as much as you admire others and you will have taken a long step toward a brighter, healthier self-image.

Every morning when you wake, read quickly through the entire list. Then pick out five qualities to think about that day. Remind yourself what a thoroughly nice person you are, and how lucky you are to have so many good qualities.

7. Hang in there. Maintaining, improving, and polishing your self-image is a lifelong task, a demanding task that will sometimes try your courage, your determination, and your imagination. But it is a task that, well and faithfully done, will bring you a lifetime of happiness.

MAKE YOURSELF COMFORTABLE

Cheerful living quarters, no matter how simple, no matter how temporary, will help you survive this difficult time. If you're more at home with people around, move in with (or near) friends or relatives, but make sure that you have a space of your own, the privacy of which will be respected when its door is closed. Periods of solitude will speed your recovery from pain. If you like to cook once in a while, find a place with a stove; if you like to swim, find a place with a pool. Avoid hotels and transient spots; they will intensify your sense of rootlessness and isolation.

Stack your place with inspirational books and comic books. Read how grit and determination catapulted others to great achievements. Renew your courage through the words of charismatic leaders and your soul with the works of the poets. But life doesn't always have to be serious. Don't discount the therapeutic value of humor — comic strips, cartoons, short stories and novels, amusing plays, light verse, and best of all an old-fashioned joke book, as simple to take and as quick to provide relief as aspirin. Nothing cracks a gloomy spell like a good belly laugh. You just can't laugh and feel sorry for yourself at the same time.

Be with people, but not all the time. Be sociable. Keep in touch with old friends and make new friends. Visit them, have dinner with them, laugh with them. Enjoy being with them.

Be alone, but not all the time. Enjoy TV, but don't use it as a substitute for action. Give yourself time to think and to plan, but don't use it as an excuse to avoid friends.

Indulge yourself and don't feel guilty about it. Buy yourself an ice cream cone or a sportcoat. Pick up an unabridged dictionary or a ticket for the football game. Until you get your life back on track, avoid high-ticket indulgences, but highlight your weeks with low-ticket sparkle.

PLAN AHEAD

If you decided to drive 3,000 miles cross-country, you'd do a lot of planning before you started. You'd dig out the maps, pinpoint your destination, figure out the best route, and estimate the time required.

You now stand at a major crossroad in your life's journey, and unless you have a plan to get where you want to go, it's unlikely you'll get there. Some folks put their plans on paper, others carry them around in their heads. I recommend writing; it demands more exactness and provides a better yardstick for measuring progress.

Your Long-Term Forecast

Your long-term forecast will serve as a compass; it will establish the true north of your life, and keep you moving in that direction. As its title implies, it should identify your objectives for say, the next ten, fifteen, or twenty years. Indicate, in rough outline, how they can be accomplished; establish an overall timetable and focus your efforts on your goals. Because of the stretch of time involved and the uncertainties of the future, you should structure your forecast in broad, general terms that make allowances for the unexpected. For instance, your cross-country plan would allow for possible car repair, and your forecast should allow for possible short-term illness or unemployment.

Your Short-Term Plan

The short-term plan is, in effect, a road map of a specific, limited period of the forecast, usually a calendar year. It should nail down, month by month, the progress you can reasonably expect to make toward your long-term objectives during the specific time period it covers, and it should also lay out, project by project, how you plan to proceed. This data will keep you on target, tell you how you're doing, whether you are on time, or whether you should adjust either your activities or your plans.

IF YOU HIT FINANCIAL PROBLEMS

If your divorce, like mine, comes on top of large existing financial commitments, the added expense of the divorce can panic you. Don't let fear immobilize you.

Contact all your creditors right away. Your negotiating position may be stronger than you think. Finance men are in the business of lending money; it's what they know how to do and it's what they like to do. They don't like to deal in secondhand cars, trucks, boats, and furniture, and if you play it real straight they usually give you every break they can.

Don't wait until they contact you. By the time legal papers are served and the repossessors arrive, it's too late to negotiate, and the longer you duck the issue, the more certainly your creditors will distrust you. Explain what's happening, assure them that you will get things under control, discuss your plans with them, and ask for the time and cooperation you need. For a while your problems may look insurmountable, but most creditors cooperate when you level with them, and things will straighten themselves out sooner than you think.

TAKE CARE OF BUSINESS

Focus on your work. Give it a high priority. You need the security of a continuous income more than you need the unemployment line. If you lose your income, you may lose more than money. You may be unable to support your child or pay for the legal advice that visitation and custody actions require. Lacking these capabilities, you may lose your child.

Get to the job every day on time and ready to work. Don't let your personal problems invade your work; park them outside the office door. You can't handle both at the same time. Keep your nerves and your temper under control. Most of your associates will feel bad about your trouble. But like me and you, they have their own problems and don't want to be whipping boys for others.

Don't rush jobs through just to get them out of the way; give each one all the time and attention it requires. Don't succumb to the feeling that nothing, including your work, matters anymore. If you let go and just let your job crash, it may take you years to climb back again, and that may be too late to be of value to you or your child.

SIGN NOTHING TODAY THAT YOU CAN PUT OFF UNTIL TOMORROW

We hear a great deal about the value of literacy, and I suppose it's fine for people who know how to use reading and writing skills judiciously. But I have a friend — I think of him as semi-literate, able to write but not to read. This is an exaggeration; he can read, but he doesn't. And he can write more than just his name, but he doesn't.

But you put a piece of paper in front of him and he will sign it without question or hesitation. He's a signature collector's ideal. Put three conflicting petitions in front of him. No problem. He'll sign them all. If you tell him you're filing for bankruptcy the next day, he'll co-sign your note today. A nice guy? Great! Think ahead, does he? Never!

As I see it, he would be better off if he had never learned to hold a pen. And until you are sure you are over the shock of divorce, you'd do well to pretend you never learned to write your name, at least until you talk with your lawyer. Signing anything without his okay is like signing a release at the site of an automobile accident. After a divorce, your emotional state may be more turbulent than you realize, and later you may regret signing papers without really understanding them, or signing them for the wrong reasons or just to get it all over with. Until you're sure your head is on straight again, check everything with your lawyer. There may be certain custody or financial agreements that it would be to your advantage to sign right now, but sign nothing without first consulting your lawyer.

Chapter 3

The Case for a Parenting Partnership

Be ye therefore wise as serpents, and harmless as doves.
— Matthew 10:16

"At the time of separation, how can parents be most helpful to their children?" In response to this question, Judith S. Wallerstein, Ph.D., the noted psychologist, answered: "How parents act is important because the child needs to think of his parents as reasonable and rational people who have taken the decision to end their relationship in a careful and thoughtful way. The child needs to see the parents as people he or she admires and can emulate, as people who are putting aside their anger and who are seriously concerned about what happens to the child, and that the child will not be forgotten. Children are very afraid they will be forgotten."[1]

YOUR CHOICE: WAR OR PEACE

You have a clearcut choice: warfare with your former spouse or the welfare of your child. Only you can make this choice, and only you can make your choice work.

If you choose to continue your warfare with your child's mother, you can turn your child into a war orphan. You can choose the destructive path so many divorced fathers feel impelled towards at one time or another. You can maintain, even escalate, your war with your child's mother, but you will do so at great cost to your child's welfare.

You can deadlock your personal life in the equivalent of an international nuclear race, and with similar results. You can concentrate all your energy on getting even; demean your dignity and the dignity of your child's mother; entangle yourself and her in legal battles, wasting time and money better directed to your child's welfare; rob your child of your attention and the attention of her mother; fill your child's living space with clouds of vindictiveness and venom; and leave her as abandoned, threatened, and fearful as any war orphan, bereft of mother and father, a victim of the war between her parents.

Your second option is a child-centered parenting partnership with your former spouse, a constructive possibility that few divorced fathers see until it is too late.

Before the marital war began, you and your former spouse had an all-encompassing partnership based on a broad spectrum of mutual interests. That partnership still exists, but it has narrowed down to a single objective: the present and future welfare of your child. Think of it as being joint executors of a trust fund for your daughter. Whether you like it or not, whether your former wife likes it or not, the two of you have a joint and equal good-faith responsibility for your child. You don't have to love your former wife in order to form a successful parenting partnership. You don't even have to like her. You do have to respect her, and you do have to establish and maintain a realistic working relationship with her in your child's interest. I hear you scream: "That's impossible! It can't be done! You don't know that witch!"

Yeah, right! And she's probably saying the same about you, with no better justification. It's the old I'm-Right-She's-Wrong, Post-Divorce, Finger-Pointing syndrome, a childish irresponsible game, degrading to players, boring to listeners.

A UNILATERAL APPROACH

A marriage partnership is similar in many ways to a business partnership. I became aware of this when I recently lunched with Al, a long-time friend, who runs a small business from which I occasionally buy parts and supplies. I hadn't seen him in some time and, while we waited for our lunch, I remarked that he was looking great, younger than he had. "You're right," he replied, "I finally resolved a people-problem that's been nagging me."

This, briefly, is Al's account of his people-problem. Sometime back, he had ended his partnership with Jimmy. Al liked Jimmy, as did everyone else, but the partnership was no longer working, and Al saw it could not go on. When he broached the subject, Jimmy was surprised and shaken, but they made a fair split and went their separate ways. Al never doubted the wisdom or the necessity of the breakup; it was better for both of them. But very little in life is 100%. Al could never quite eradicate a subtle feeling of guilt for having chosen business pragmatism over personal loyalty in ending the partnership, and he still missed Jimmy. Sometimes, as staff meetings droned on, Jimmy's face came unbidden to mind, jaw-clenched and determined when their bank declined their loan application, or exuberant with the joy of placing their first really big order, the one that put them on their feet and kept them in business. It seemed that the business was no longer any fun; all the humor and glitter and adventure had packed up and left with Jimmy.

Later, some remarks Jimmy had made, spiteful and rancorous, drifted back through business associates. He knew how to hit Al where it would hurt, right on top of existing bruises. His well-aimed punches landed, as his knowledge of Al had told him they would, smash on top of Al's nostalgia about their "early days," and his ambiguity about the business breakup.

Al retaliated by hurling back equally hurtful remarks through the business grapevine, and he enjoyed the satisfaction of knowing that they would reach Jim, and that they would sting. The feud continued, the remarks turned from cutting to vicious, until a friend of Al's pointed out that Al and Jimmy had become a laughingstock by constantly trying to justify a past that few remembered and none cared about. Al, recalling how other businessmen had degraded themselves and their partners by petty public criticism of each other, recognized the truth and acted.

He reversed his tactics and began talking about Jim's fine qualities. Word got back to Jim, and his comments about Al slowly became less biting, then turned friendly, and that morning, just before we met for lunch, an order had come across Al's desk, a small order of no consequence to the business, but of great significance to Al — an order from Jimmy, the first he had placed with Al since their split.

Puzzlement skewed Al's smile as he finished the story. He looked up from the table and shook his head. "Funny," he said, "the things we do when we're hurt. What drives us to hurt the other person so we'll feel better? What makes us feverishly try to prove that we are right and the other person is wrong? Everything we do brings the reverse of what we really want. We hurt others; they retaliate; the hurt increases. We seek public approval by proclaiming our virtues, and we make ourselves look ridiculous and lose what respect we had."

Then he added, in a more thoughtful tone, "There are better, saner ways. Hurt people don't have to hurt people."

Sound familiar? The sniping, the accusations. The exaggeration of your virtues, the amplification of your former wife's faults. The desperate need to prove that you're a martyr and she's a witch. Why do we plead our case to anyone who will listen, when actually, the world doesn't care?

Al was right. Bickering and name calling explode into self-perpetuating hostility. There is a better way, a unilateral approach to peace. Al made it work for him, and you can make it work for you, too. With patience and resolve you can bring peace — with all its miraculous potential for personal growth and prosperity — into the life of your child, into the life of your child's mother, and into your own life.

There come moments shortly after a divorce when each party feels driven to explain to the world how he was right and she was wrong, or she was right and he was wrong. Don't succumb to the feeling. Don't "tell a friend." No matter how rigid your integrity, this is one time you will color the picture slightly in your desperate need to protect both your self-image and your public image. And when it is relayed to your former wife, and it will be, the messenger will add more color. And the picture, when delivered, will strike like a slap across the face. To retaliate, she will present her slightly colored picture of you, the blazing duel escalates, and both of you look pretty silly.

Few among us have escaped the divorce courts, and even fewer are without friends or family members who have escaped. In most regions of the United States, divorce is neither a scandal nor a disgrace. It's just a fact of life, a dull, unpleasant fact of life to which we are so accustomed it has lost its power to interest or startle. Recognize the fact that the world doesn't see you as a monster or a failure. Accept the fact that the world really doesn't care much about your divorce. It's the first step to regaining total mental health.

CARE AND MAINTENANCE OF THE CHILD-CENTERED PARENTS' PARTNERSHIP

It would be nice if you could put this decision off until you overcome emotional stress and recapture your balance. There is, unfortunately, no time to waste. The longer you put it off, the more deeply you will become entrenched in battle, the harder it will be to change, the more certain your failure.

Don't wait until the time is right; it's as right now as it will ever be. Make your decision today and get started. It's a lot to ask of you when you are going through what will probably be the most stressful period of your life, but your child's welfare is in the balance.

Keep Your Eye on Your Goal

Keep all discussions with your former wife centered on the problem and in the present. Don't let them slide over into another subject or slip back into the past. Your parenting partnership has only one goal, the welfare of your child. Keep it in mind at all times; lose sight of it and you wander aimless as a tourist without a road map.

Be Responsible

Keep your former wife informed as to where you can be reached in emergencies. Fulfill your financial obligations; pay her everything due her by mutual agreement or court order, on time and in full. Be on time for all appointments with her or your child.

Don't make one-sided decisions on questions in which she is entitled to a voice. Aside from the fact that it's unfair, it could lead to her making decisions without consulting you.

If you have something to say, say it to her; don't assign your child the uncomfortable position of messenger. Make all communications, either written or oral, clear, exact, and complete.

Respect Your Child's Mother and Demand Respect for Yourself

Respect, a fundamental right of every human being, is the soundest foundation on which to build a successful partnership. In addition, regardless of the differences between you and your former wife, she is entitled to the respect due her as the mother of your child; when you insult her, you insult your child. More importantly, when you fail to respect her and her rights, you fail your child by decreasing the quality of care and guidance the mother provides.

Give your child's mother the same courtesy you give your child's teacher or doctor. In effect, she is both — and far more. Not only does she supervise the child's education and health, she dominates the emotional and philosophical world in which the child spends much of her time.

I do business with a man — we'll call him Harvey — a bright enough person, but he can't see beyond his nose when it comes to his former wife; the sound of her name sends him into a rage. Like some people do crossword puzzles, he sits and devises ways to annoy her and, when he succeeds, he's as jubilant as if he had completed a *New York Times* puzzle in record time. As concerned as he is about his children's welfare, he can't see that, when he upsets their mother, he reduces her ability to take care of the children. Don't make his mistake. Your child will have to pay for it.

The comments above apply equally to you. As an individual and as the child's father, you also are entitled to respect. If you don't insist on that respect, you will diminish your effectiveness as a parent and as a father-figure. Being a nice guy is one thing; letting anyone walk all over you is another.

Be Flexible

There are times you should not compromise, but they are few: 1) When it will harm your child, your child's mother, yourself, or anyone else; 2) When it will violate principle, ethics, or morality; and 3) When it's impossible. Otherwise, make any reasonable compromise to promote the happiness, convenience, or welfare of your child or her mother. Don't expect immediate and enthusiastic compromise in return; be satisfied with anything short of stubborn obstruction. Generally, cooperation begets cooperation. But don't bank on it; sometimes it begets more demands. Regardless of the response, continue to be at least reasonably cooperative. Decreasing stress in your child's life will be the real payoff.

CONFERENCES THAT WORK

Plan Ahead

Before you call or meet your former spouse, prepare a written note of the items to discuss. It will organize your ideas, keep you on the subject, and help you cover everything you have in mind.

The new "limited" nature of your partnership requires a new formality. Your former spouse, like you, is entitled to privacy; showing up unannounced and unexpected violates her privacy. A rule of thumb: always call and make an appointment. Keep to this rule unless you have grounds to suspect that your child is inadequately supervised.

But if you are satisfied that the grounds are valid; that you are not imagining a problem where it doesn't exist; that you are not using an imaginary problem as an excuse; and that impromptu visits are necessary to ascertain the facts, then do so, but only with full and due regard to the privacy rights of all concerned.

Be Businesslike

Arrive on time, drug- and alcohol-free, clear headed, civil, and prepared to talk business. Listen carefully and keep an open mind. Try to accommodate anything that will make life easier for the mother or the child, but don't be tricked, lured, or prodded into unreasonable commitments or commitments you can't keep.

It's amazing how many people put themselves into tight spots, especially in financial matters, on the mistaken idea that they have to snap back an immediate response to every foolish question they're asked. Give yourself time to think about it, and if necessary, to run it past your lawyer. Very few questions, other than in emergencies, require an answer today; most things can hold until tomorrow. You're more apt to regret a hasty answer than a considered answer.

Don't Push the Battle Button

People who have been married acquire a knowledge of each other's likes and dislikes; they know what leads to peace and what sounds the battle cry. This knowledge can be used constructively or destructively. Some people, when an argument turns against them, reach for the battle button that will explode the other person's anger, frequently injuring the bomber as much as the bombed. It is a malicious use of private knowledge, and I'm convinced it's a major reason many post-divorce wrangles, once they take root, are as tenaciously self-propagating as weeds.

Some people, however, skillfully exploit the peace-keeping advantages of their knowledge to restore and maintain peace. Let me recommend that you follow the latter course; spare yourself the ravages and expenses of war. You may miss the momentary elation of winning pointless battles, but you will know the joy of winning wars, wars against your own vindictive instincts, and wars for your child's welfare.

Keep the Conference Cool

When your former wife turns the conference table into a battlefield, stay calm. Refuse to be tricked into an emotional confrontation. Ignore personal remarks and thinly veiled hostility. They are only invitations to argue. Sidestep them and get back to the point under discussion.

There's no surefire way to stand clear of the argument and move the meeting on. Sometimes it helps to ignore the outburst and get on with the problem; occasionally it's necessary to take a stand and refuse to discuss a matter that's irrelevant to the problem under discussion. Other times it works to slowly lower your voice until she has to stop screaming in order to hear what you're saying or, if tempers (yours and/or hers) get out of hand, leave and discuss it later.

Whatever tactic you take, execute it quietly and deliberately. Every peaceful conference leads to further peaceful conferences. But once you shatter the peace, you have to start all over again, and with a higher probability of stormy conferences.

Concentrate on creating and maintaining the child-centered parenting partnership, and make it work for all of you.

Chapter 4

Child Custody
and Visitation

*Our findings regarding the centrality of both parents to
the psychological health of the children and adolescents
alike leads us to hold that, where possible, divorcing parents should be encouraged and helped to shape post divorce arrangements which permit and foster continuity in
the children's relation with both parents.*

— Judith S. Wallerstein and Joan Berlin Kelly,
Surviving the Breakup [1]

As divorce increases, psychological studies of its effect on the family,
especially on the children, also increase. Study after study documents
the beneficial effect a continuing association with both parents exerts
on children. The Hetherington, Cox, and Cox studies find that, when
mothers have sole custody, fathers begin to detach emotionally from
the children during the first year of divorce and, as the bond weakens, they see the children less and less. Two years after the divorce,
fewer than half of the ninety-six fathers in the study saw their children as often as once a week, although they lived nearby. [2]

Hetherington and her colleagues observe that, when fathers
maintain frequent contact with the family, children adjust better and
aren't as apt to develop the aggressive, immature behavior frequently
characteristic of children who have minimal contact with their fathers. Wallerstein and Kelly find that frequent visits with fathers
help young children overcome the self-blame they often feel about the
divorce. [3] Shinn's study demonstrates that children do better in
school when fathers visit frequently. [4] Biller and Davids observe that
sons who see their fathers infrequently tend to act immaturely; relate
poorly to their peers; and either fail to develop masculine traits or
make exaggerated attempts to prove their masculinity. [5] Hess and
Camara observed that the child's adjustment greatly improves when
he maintains an intimate relationship with both parents. [6]

These opinions which, in general, reflect the findings of researchers, are consistent with those of professionals — judges, child psychologists, social workers, and teachers — who work with children every day.

And they confirm what we, as divorced fathers, know in our hearts: we are every bit as important to our children as they are to us.

Hold that thought in mind while we look at custody, its history, where it is today, and what we can do about it.

HISTORY OF CUSTODY

First came the "Chattel Theory." Under England's medieval common law, which forms the basis of United States law, the early American father owned his children, just as he owned his furniture and livestock; they were his "chattel," his personal, legal possessions, just as the farm and the farm house were his real property. The mother had no legal right to children or property. When parents divorced, the father kept his farm and his house, and he also kept his children, regardless of their ages, his fitness to raise them, or the reason for the divorce.

In response to the harshness of this practice, the "Tender Years Doctrine" slowly evolved. Neither children nor mothers gained any legal rights or means of legal redress, but the infants' need for maternal nurturing was as obvious as the inhumanity of tearing them from their mothers' arms, and courts — in the absence of any clear evidence that mothers were "unfit" — began awarding them custody of children of "tender years."

In the late 1800s the Tender Years doctrine expanded and solidified into a "Mother as Caretaker, Father as Breadwinner" pattern. The industrial revolution, which had changed America from an agricultural to an industrial society, had also changed the pattern of family life. Jane still stayed at home, did the housework, and took care of the children. But Dick no longer worked a farm; he earned the family living at the local mill. Both the mother and the father still had full-time jobs. A popular maxim of the time accurately states, "Man works from sun to sun. A woman's work is never done." The mother had good strong brown soap, a scrub board, a hand wringer to roll the clothes through, and a foot treadle machine to mend them on; she had no time to help earn the family living. The father labored ten to eleven hours a day, six days a week, not counting the time it took him to walk to the mill every day; he had no time to help with the cooking, the washing, and the children.

So when the rare divorce occurred, neither mother nor father changed the nature or place of their work. The mother remained in the family home, and continued to take care of the children.

The father, unlike preceding generations of men who had worked the land, moved out of the home but continued his work at the then new place of employment for men, the mill. The mother retained the home, the furniture, and the children. The father, still required to support the home from which he was exiled, was divested of all rights, especially those pertaining to his children.

The only way a father could win custody of his children was to prove that the mother was unfit to take care of them. But ironically, divorce frequently closed that path to him. In those pre-dissolution days with no such thing as "no fault," adultery was one of the few grounds for divorce, and it was considered "gentlemanly" for the husband to take the blame. Only a cad or a very bitter husband would publicly accuse the mother of his children of adultery, so — and it was commonly known — evidence of a husband's adultery was often fraudulently contrived to meet the court's requirements. Consequently, although the husband was often blameless, he was, in the eyes of the court, technically guilty of adultery which automatically made him an unfit father and precluded his getting custody.

In the 1870s woman's position was further strengthened by the right to hold property, and in 1920 by the right to vote. But the tumultuous changes came in the late 1940s. New birth control methods freed her from unplanned motherhood; industry, flooding her with reasonably priced energy-saving devices, freed her from round-the-clock-housework; diversified post-war sex roles freed her from traditional female occupations; and offices and factories, for which she had worked during World War II, welcomed her back.

Many men — especially those of us who have daughters and evaluate the changing times in terms of their expanding opportunities — feel that women's new rights, new freedoms, and new options are long overdue. Even as we wince at our loss of privilege, we applaud a new day that promises to redress the imbalance of opportunity between our sons and our daughters.

We do, however, bitterly protest the courts' unfounded preference to women in awarding child custody. Exclusion from custody, especially of a daughter but also of a son, inhibits a man's ability to serve as guide or mentor; to help prepare them for tomorrow's opportunities; to share with them his knowledge of trade, commerce, industry, politics, and professions gleaned over the longer period during which men have worked outside the home, and which, traditionally, men have handed down to sons. The time, but not the opportunity, has come for men to hand this knowledge down to their daughters.

Fortunately, custody is tending somewhat toward the father, despite an occasional court ruling against our interests. Courts, recognizing that a child needs both parents, are broadening the father's custodial rights. Many courts feel that equally "fit" parents should share equal custody of the children. And three powerful forces currently assist men's struggle for broader custodial rights: the first is the exemplary parenting demonstrated by many custodial fathers. The second, the strong educational and political efforts of fathers' groups such as Fathers for Equal Rights and Equal Rights for Fathers. The third, paradoxically, is the women's movement. It has so effectively encouraged women to take control of their own and their children's lives; to obtain stressful, demanding jobs; to be independent and self sufficient, that many overworked, overloaded, overstressed women openly welcome, indeed demand, parenting help from fathers.

The automatic presumption that mothers are better able to care for children has been eradicated from most state laws. But it has not been written out of the general American consciousness. Even judges, humanly susceptible to conscious and unconscious bias, get snagged by the stereotype that only a mother can bake a real apple pie or comfort an unhappy child. And the lingering, covert presumption is that women, by virtue of being women, are better parents. The courts' tendency to give them preference in custodial matters will not disappear overnight, and will not disappear at all unless men acquire their equal custodial rights and fulfill their custodial responsibilities equally.

CHILD CUSTODY

When reading the following overview on child custody, please keep in mind that it cannot deal with the details of the hundreds of jurisdictions in the United States; for specifics as they apply to your interests, check with your local court or your lawyer.

Child custody is any of several forms of legal guardianship of a specific child, awarded by a court to an individual or individuals, usually the father or mother.

Forms of Custody and How They Work

Each individual state controls child custody within its own borders. The forms of custody, therefore, can vary from state to state and from jurisdiction to jurisdiction, but in general, they are similar to those described below. Your lawyer or the clerk of the court having jurisdiction in your case can give you precise information about the forms of custody in that jurisdiction.

De Facto Custody vs. De Jure Custody

Parents share legal and physical responsibility for a child, and this shared responsibility continues, unless changed by a court, even when a child lives with only one parent. But, during the disintegration of a marriage, there usually comes a time (from the moment one of the parents leaves until the moment the court issues a temporary custody order), when the child is really under the exclusive care of one parent. This parent becomes the actual or de facto (in fact) custodian, until the court designates a legal or de jure (in law) custodian.

If, as frequently occurs, the mother and child stay in the home and the father has to move out, the father's absence, by leaving the child under the mother's control, automatically makes the mother the actual, or de facto, custodian. Usually neither parent is aware at the time that de facto custodianship will become an advantage to the custodian and a disadvantage to the non-custodian.

Then comes the question of temporary custody. The judge, in deciding which parent will be a better single parent, compares the experience and qualifications of the applicants. The strategic importance of de facto custody begins to emerge at this point. The father has no single-parent experience, whereas, the mother as a de facto custodian is a single parent, and her experience is relevant. If this experience was anything short of disastrous, and if she is otherwise fit, the judge usually awards her temporary custody, and throws in occupancy of the homestead so the child can remain in a familiar environment. The father, lulled by the throwaway sound of "temporary," accepts the rejection of his application, feeling that he can easily get it straightened out in the permanent order.

Then comes the permanent order. And things get worse. Temporary custody has increased the mother's single-parent experience and, without such experience, the father cannot effectively contend for custody. Overwhelming deja vu grips him as he relives the dilemma of early years when he couldn't get a job without experience, and he couldn't get experience without a job.

Every passing day strengthens the mother's position and weakens the father's. Earlier it would have been enough to demonstrate that he would be a "better" custodian. But it's too late for that now. If the child is being "responsibly" supervised, a judge will not arbitrarily remove the custodian in order to appoint a potentially superior custodian; one of his paramount objectives is to maintain the stability of a child who has been traumatized by divorce-generated changes. It is similar to an office situation: few employers will fire an adequate employee to hire a superior (maybe) employee. To obtain a change, the father must present evidence that the mother is unfit and that the child is subjected to detrimental or dangerous conditions. Such a path, even if successful, will risk psychological damage to the child and the child's mother, and will cost thousands of dollars and endless hours in court. The father could have avoided the entire problem and given himself an even chance, if he had been alert to the significance of de facto custody from the onset.

Let me urge you to stay alert to the danger of "unofficial" arrangements becoming "temporary" and turning into "permanent" custody restrictions you'll have to live with. If you are sure you know the conditions you want, try to structure them into the de facto custody so they'll have a good chance of being written into the temporary, and then into the permanent, custody order.

If you're still devastated by the divorce, disoriented and uncertain about what you want and how much you can handle, try — at the very least — to keep the terms of the temporary order flexible.

Temporary Custody

Courts customarily give temporary custody to one parent, usually the mother, to insure the child's welfare during the divorce proceedings; this order is replaced by a permanent order of custody at the end of the trial.

Sole Legal Custody

In sole legal custody, one person, usually the father or mother, has sole right to make all decisions, major and minor, affecting the growth and development of the child, including health, education, religion, and residence. For example, the sole legal custodian can, independently, transfer the child from one school to another, or from one form of religious training to another.

Shared Legal Custody

Shared legal custody gives more than one person, usually the mother and father, joint responsibility for making all decisions affecting the growth and development of the child. Neither the father alone nor the mother alone can, for example transfer the child from one school to another, or from one form of religious training to another.

If you are not in a position to, or prefer not to, make all legal decisions, let me recommend that you discuss shared legal custody with your lawyer. It has advantages. It provides the child with two adult guardians instead of one, and in the event of the illness or death of one custodian, the other is familiar with the child's life situation, and can step in immediately to assist. You would not have total control, but you would always have veto power.

Sole Physical Custody

In sole physical custody, the child lives full-time with one person, usually a parent, or at any other place the custodian may designate (such as a boarding school). The court can give visiting rights to the other parent, either at his residence or the child's full-time residence, or another place.

Shared Physical Custody

In shared physical custody, the child lives part-time with each custodian. For example, half a year with each parent; school months with one parent, vacations with the other; alternate weeks or months with each parent; or weekdays with one parent, weekends with the other. In shared physical custody, the child is not a family member at one home and a visitor at the other as in sole physical custody. He's a family member at both homes. This arrangement is both good and bad. The child doesn't have to adjust to a complete break with either parent, but on the other hand, he lacks a solid, continuous relationship with either.

In this type of custody, the distance between the two homes becomes of obvious importance. If you can afford jet fares and your child doesn't suffer from jet lag or fear of flying; if Thanksgiving in San Diego and Christmas in Boston is no problem; if you can command the time and transportation to get to your child's side in an emergency, then you can probably handle joint physical custody. Otherwise, logistics and finances can present insurmountable problems.

For shared physical custody you will need a statement showing the feasibility of your plan and how it will affect the quality of your child's life. Go over it carefully and make sure it will work; you can be sure the judge will examine it in detail. As a general rule, the simpler the plan, the more convenient for all, the more favorably the court will receive it. Generally it works out better if both parents live in the same geographic area, and if possible, in the same school district.

WHO DECIDES CUSTODY AND VISITATION QUESTIONS?

Divorce is the legal dissolution of a marriage contract by a court of law. The judge makes all decisions relating to the divorce, including the custody of children. But I want to be very specific about the judge's responsibility, because it can sound misleading.

To say that the judge makes the decisions is not to say that he does so in isolation. In determining the child's best interests and assessing the fitness of parents to act as custodians, he may consult with the mother, father, family members, neighbors, employers, doctors, psychologists, social workers, and teachers. In arriving at custody and visitation decisions, he may consider proposals from the mother, father, family members, court mediators, and arbitrators. But all of this is "input."

After he considers all "input," he writes a court order stipulating who will have custody, what kind it will be, and who will have visiting rights. This is his "decision."

Five Ways to Reach a Custody/Visitation Plan

Most courts offer at least five different ways to arrive at custody and visitation plans:

Option 1: Plan Presented by Both Parents
Option 2: Mediation Services
Option 3: Court Mediator
Option 4: Binding Arbitration
Option 5: Court Decision

Option 1 gives you and your spouse virtually full control and each subsequent option chips away at that control until Option 5 takes the matter right out of your hands. Try to make Option 1 work; it will make both your life and that of your child more pleasant.

OPTION 1: Plan Presented by Both Parents

You and your spouse agree on a custody and visitation plan before the case comes to the courtroom. Most judges, recognizing that custody involves sensitive psychological forces best known to the parents, encourage them to formulate their own plan. And if it doesn't violate the best interests of the child, a judge usually accepts and incorporates it into the court order without change.

Disadvantage: None

Advantage: Option 1, usually the hardest to achieve, is also the simplest, most economical, and most comfortable for everyone. By decreasing hostility between parents, it makes the child's life happier. It protects him from being mangled in court procedures, and it spares him the pain of choosing between parents. It saves the court's time, and conserves your time and money which can be more profitably directed to your child's welfare. Parents who set aside their personal differences and work out a fair plan should be very proud of themselves.

OPTION 2: Mediation Services

Mediation is voluntary in most jurisdictions, and it is usually offered at nominal or no cost. Skilled mediators, professionals knowledgeable in domestic law, help both of you reach agreement. They maintain an impartial attitude, help establish priorities, separate problems so you can consider them a step at a time, suggest pragmatic alternatives and mutually acceptable trade-offs, get you through the gridlocks, and encourage creative compromises.

You, not the mediation service, make all the decisions. You can, if you wish, decide that no decision is possible, in which case the court refers you to the court mediator, where you run the risk of having the decision made for you.

If, on the other hand, the two of you reach a decision, the judge generally accords it the same consideration he would have given an Option 1 plan, and incorporates it in his court order.

Disadvantage: Option 2 contains no absolute disadvantage, only the threat of a disadvantage, the awareness that this may be your last chance to do it your way. If, however, you and your spouse work out an acceptable plan, you will achieve everything Option 1 could have given you.

Advantage: Option 2 is a second chance, and many parents who haven't agreed on anything in years achieve wondrous accord under the pressure of their decreasing options.

OPTION 3: Court Mediator

If issues remain unresolved, the court refers you to a court mediator, a professional and experienced counselor. The three of you meet privately, without any lawyers present. The court mediator, like the mediation service, tries to help you reach agreement. He clarifies the issues, deals with the important concerns, discourages petty bickering, and keeps you centered on the goal.

If you agree on a plan, the court mediator commits it to writing and submits it to the judge, who usually incorporates it in his court order just as it is. If, however, you fail to agree, you lose control over the situation. The court mediator makes his own recommendations, with which you may or may not agree, and which the judge will probably include in his court order.

Disadvantage: You have a fifty-fifty chance of losing control of the situation, and being given a plan you didn't design and probably don't like.

Advantage: You have a fifty-fifty chance of winning. And if you win, you win everything; your terms will most probably appear in the court order exactly as you state them.

OPTION 4: Binding Arbitration

If you don't want to accept the court mediator's plan, binding arbitration provides an additional, if limited, alternative. You can request that an unbiased third party hear both sides of the unresolved dispute between you and your wife, and make a decision. This decision, which will be binding, is submitted to the judge for consideration and if he accepts it, it is included in the final order.

Disadvantage: You have no direct control over the outcome; no way to predict it; whatever it is, you have to accept either the court order or the expense and pain of custody battles.

Advantage: Short of a court fight, it's your last chance to influence, however indirectly, the official custody terms.

OPTION 5: Court Decision

You're out of the action at this point. If you have gone through binding arbitration, the results of the arbitration will become effective. If you have bypassed arbitration, the judge now decides the custody terms.

Disadvantage: If you can't accept the judge's plan, your only alternative is to fight it out in court.

Advantage: Even if you don't like the terms of custody, you can be sure that the judge will have made a carefully considered decision which, in his educated and experienced opinion, will be in the best interests of your child.

"THE BEST INTERESTS OF THE CHILD"

The United States, where each individual state establishes its own custody laws, is one of the few modern countries that lacks nationwide custody legislation. The nearest we come to a national standard is the principle of "The Best Interests of the Child." Custody practices may differ from court to court, but the broad areas of agreement encompassed by this principle apply from coast to coast.

"The Best Interests of the Child," unlike the United States Constitution, is not a nationwide formal, legal document. It is much like England's 13th century unwritten, but universally understood, common law — an informal, flexible, and widely used guideline. It pulls together a set of conditions intended to protect a child's safety, and foster his happiness, adjustment, and development. It concentrates on the rights, not of parents, but of their children.

How Does the Judge Determine
"The Best Interests of the Child"?

If, tomorrow, you and I face the near certainty of dying within the month, our immediate concern would be to place our children in good hands. We have no rigid guideline. No exact formula. No standards of weights and measures. Nothing but common sense and a crystal ball. Our first act would probably be to mentally list all the people who might willingly undertake so major a responsibility. From this list, we would strike anyone lacking the necessary physical, mental, or financial capacity, and those who, by the very fact of being themselves, constitute a hazard to a child's safety, such as child molesters.

We now have a list of people who are "fit" to be custodians, from which we must select the "most fit," a determination requiring sensitive understanding of the child's needs and an accurate evaluation of a prospective custodian's abilities to meet these needs. For any given child, your selection may differ from mine, but we will arrive at our selections by much the same mental process, and we both will have been guided by the best interests of the children.

The process by which a judge selects a custodian, although more formal, is essentially similar to ours. Technically, he is guided by case law (previous court decisions), written law, local customs, mores, and the practices of his individual court. But guidelines frequently refuse to fit snugly within the tangled and mercurial facts of a custody case, and the judge is thrown back on the same common sense, crystal ball, and "best interests of the child" on which we rely.

Some states issue their own written interpretations of the "best interests of the child" which a judge must consider when making custody decisions. Some courts which have no statewide directives, prepare written statements for their own guidance, and some courts apply the principle without a written guide.

How to Make "The Best Interests of the Child" Work for You

First, let me suggest that you ask your court for a copy of its "best interests of the child" policy. It can be helpful because:

1. Divorce and custody aside, it contains a thought-provoking perspective on child raising; some of it obvious (a child needs love and understanding), some not so obvious (wealth can impede, rather than foster, a child's development).

2. It dissipates some of the mystery about court proceedings. When you know what the judge is trying to find out, you understand his questions more quickly and are better able to answer them.

3. It sharpens your awareness of the court's view of your conduct and, in some instances, gives you an opportunity to shape your conduct to its standards.

4. When you understand what the court considers important, your documentation will be stronger. The more specific your knowledge, the stronger your position. If specific knowledge is unavailable, general knowledge is better than none. As I mentioned before, details vary from state to state but the basic concepts remain fairly consistent.

Important Points of "The Best Interests" Principle

SAFETY
Focus:
Elimination of hazards to the child arising from unfitness of custodian.
Evidence the Court Considers:
PHYSICAL HEALTH — The physical care of children, especially very young children, requires tremendous energy and endurance. The judge knows from experience that parents, especially those who have previously shared child-rearing with the other parent and don't know how strenuous twenty-four hour a day responsibility can be, seldom realize the magnitude of the burden they seek. He must, therefore, consider the adequacy of a prospective custodian's health.

Custody Implications: The judge does not look for world-class athletic condition, just the ability to get the job done. He knows that the blind, the mute, the deaf, and the physically handicapped have been successful custodians. He does not deny custody on the basis of an isolated physical deficiency, but he wants to know if you can adequately compensate for any deficiency so the child's welfare will not be compromised.

Don't let a physical restriction deter you from requesting custody. But be prepared to present evidence that you can fulfill all the child's needs. Build a clearcut case. State exactly how you plan to supplement your personal efforts by professional assistance, special facilities or equipment, household help, cooperating family members, or community services.

Attach supporting statements from health professionals and anyone else who has knowledge of the situation or who will participate in the child's care.

MENTAL HEALTH — Safeguarding children requires a deep and constant sense of responsibility, sound judgment, stability, and the rationality to recognize and deal with hazards that threaten a child's psychological and physiological well-being. The judge must assure himself that the custodian meets these requirements.

Custody Implications: A long history of reckless, irresponsible behavior, drug dependence, child abuse, sexual abuse, or chronic psychotic episodes characterized by violence or aberrant behavior can pretty obviously disqualify you. But mental illness or psychiatric hospitalization, of themselves, do not necessarily do so, especially if you have recovered.

The court is concerned with your past life only as it affects the child's present and future life. Keep this in mind when you document your case. Provide complete data about the problem, its duration, treatment, current status, and prognosis. Emphasize your ability to take excellent care of the child now and in the future. Statements from mental health professionals are essential.

MORALITY — More than any other person, the custodian serves as a guide for moral standards and a role model for social adaptation. The court evaluates the virtues and vices of prospective custodians as demonstrated by their conduct, in the light of community standards, to determine how they would affect the child.

Courts differ in the importance they place on any specific aspect of morality, but most of them frown on antisocial activities; public brawling or repeated conflicts with the law; intemperate use of alcohol or drugs; extramarital promiscuity; inappropriate sexual behavior in the presence of children; history of serious financial or credit problems; and behavior so different from the community standards that it would jeopardize a child's acceptance by the community.

Custody Implications: A historian once said: If you make a great heap of everything that people at some time or some place thought was right, and withdraw from that heap everything that people at some time or some place thought was wrong, you will have nothing left.

Evaluation of morality has never been an exact science, but it's becoming increasingly ambiguous. Relatively few years ago, any American court routinely adjudged any adulterous wife to be a "fallen woman" and, ipso facto, an "unfit" custodian. Custody award automatically went to the father. We have come a long way. Sometimes it's hard to discern in what direction, but we have come a long way.

In today's courts, morality standards range from uncompromisingly conservative to unrelentingly liberal. Behavior acceptable in one section of the country can disqualify you as a custodian in another. If you are fortunate enough to retain an experienced custody lawyer who is familiar with local courts, he can tell you how most of the local judges lean. Follow his advice.

STABILITY AND CONTINUITY

Focus:

Maximum stability and continuity of home, environment, and people in the child's life.

Evidence the Court Considers:

THE HOME — Before a court makes or changes a custody award, it considers the stability of the child's present home and how long he has been there. If the supervision is satisfactory and no unusual problems appear, the court usually prefers to let the child remain where he is.

Custody Implications: Courts prefer that a child remain in one home and not be shifted about from one place to another. They find that permanence of surroundings — the same neighborhood play-mates, the same school, the same furniture, books, and toys — gives the child a stable base from which he can deal more effectively with the other changes in his life.

THE CUSTODIAN — The court compares the quality of love, affection, personal relationship, and emotional ties between the child and the present custodian with that existing between the child and the non-custodian, including mutual respect, companionship, communication, understanding, warmth, and concern.

Custody Implications: This appears to be an even-handed comparison of the child's relationship with each of the parents, and may the best man win. But it's not that simple. An advantage goes to the custodian with whom the child lives, because the qualities considered in this area are the very qualities that can flourish between people who live together. When the judge examines the relationship between the child and the custodian, he examines the product of their living together, but when he examines the relationship between the child and the non-custodian, there is nothing to examine because there was no opportunity for it to develop.

The custodian with whom the child lives has an all but unbeatable advantage.

FAMILY UNIT — To avoid bouncing the child around from group to group, courts try to place him in the family unit with the highest probability of permanency. The size of the family units, which can range from parent-and-child to sprawling commune, substantially affects the scope of the court's investigation. If each family unit limits itself to parent and child, only the comparative intent and ability of the individual parents to maintain a permanent family unit need be examined.

If, however, either or both of the family units includes others such as friends, relatives, or prospective spouses, the court considers the influence of these additional people on the permanence and character of the group. If either the father or mother has a new or prospective spouse, the stability of that person and the stability of the relationship between that person and the parent become important factors. A record of frequent police intervention to investigate altercations or quell fights could easily cost a parent custody of a child.

Custody Implications: The custodial parent has a distinct head start. Her time as a single parent demonstrates her intent and ability to maintain a permanent family unit; the non-custodial parent lacks similar experience.

GUIDANCE

Evidence the Court Considers:

EDUCATION — In the absence of any special need a judge usually concentrates, not on the parents' academic records, but on their attitude toward the child's education and their ability to provide academic encouragement and guidance. If the child is of school age, the judge investigates the parents' past involvement in his education. Did they, one or both, encourage him? Did they keep a close eye on his progress? Did they know when he needed help? Did they work with him or obtain tutorial help when needed? Attend parent-teacher conferences?

Custody Implications: The judge favors a custodian who can recognize learning difficulties and deal with them before they become disabling; who will be aware of special abilities and the options they give the child; and who will support the child in the level and area of learning best suited to his desires and abilities.

If you acquire the knowledge to perform these functions, you might, one day, influence a judge in your favor. More importantly, you would know how to guide your child's educational activities, one of the most important and lasting influences of his entire life. The knowledge is available to you in your local bookstore or the reference room of your public library.

RELIGION — Judges do not distinguish between religions. They concern themselves about the merits of a specific religion only when it poses a potential threat to the child, as do certain radical cults.

But if religion is important in the child's life, if it contributes to his identity or his development, most judges favor the parent who can encourage continuation of the child's usual religious practices which, if the mother and father are of different religions, is logically the parent of the same religion as the child.

Custody Implications: Religion seldom constitutes a primary custody issue, but when it does it can explode into bitterness. Emotional outbursts and theological defenses of a specific religion will not sway the judge; he seeks only to establish permanence and continuity in the child's life.

Even if you are not of the same religion as the child, even if you have no religion, don't give up. Be prepared to show how you will support the child's religious activity. Stress the fact that you can respect and encourage the child's belief without sharing it.

MONEY

Focus:

Adequate provision of the child's basic material necessities.

Evidence the Court Considers:

The court examines the financial situation of each parent, and determines how and by whom food, clothing, education, medical expenses, and other basic material necessities can best be provided. It evaluates the capability and the willingness of each parent, as demonstrated by past and present performance, to participate in the child's support.

If one parent has significantly higher income, the court considers whether living with that parent would be an advantage to the child. But few courts rate wealth, beyond an amount sufficient to assure the child's needs, of any great value to the child. In fact, many courts question excessive spending; too many times they have seen it used to buy a child's love, a practice they deem detrimental to the child.

Custody Implications: Money, as such, seldom influences custody decisions. Courts merely want to be sure that the child's basic needs are met, and to decide how much the non-custodial parent should participate in providing for them.

The personal qualities we discussed above — love, affection, guidance — depend on close contact with the child; therefore, those qualities confer an advantage. Money is different. Its obligations do not require physical closeness; they can be handled by checks paid directly to the supermarket, the department store, the school, and the hospital. It follows that, since the ability to pay bills does not require physical closeness to the child, the court seldom accords it much weight in deciding physical custody awards.

The fact is that you should not expect custodial preference on the basis of financial superiority.

CHILD'S PREFERENCE

Focus:

Taking into consideration with which parent the child prefers to live.

Evidence the Court Considers:

Judges consider, but are not bound by, a child's preference. They must determine not only what the child wants, but also what is best for him. An infant or very young child lacks the communication and reasoning skills to form and express a valid choice; an older child, while he may articulate his choice well, may lack the maturity to choose in his own best interests. Judges feel a child can usually make an informed choice at fourteen or fifteen and the older the child is, the more weight the judge accords his preference.

Custody Implications: The judge listens to more than the child's words; he looks behind the words to find out if the child is making an immature, hedonistic choice, seeking today's pleasure at the expense of tomorrow's success. When a child prefers one parent's home because there are more games, parties, presents, and higher allowances and lower restrictions, the judge delves further to determine whether the parent is providing a happy and constructive atmosphere conducive to the child's healthy development, or trying to buy the child's favor and shirk his disciplinary and guidance responsibilities. The judge's findings in this matter will weigh heavily in determining the parent's fitness as a custodian.

NEED FOR SPECIAL CUSTODIAL CONDITIONS
Focus:
Any signs indicating need for special custodial conditions.
Evidence the Court Considers:
The custodial qualifications we have discussed so far — competence, love, guidance, money — apply equally to either parent.

Occasionally, however, a special circumstance such as impairments (mental or physical) or gifts (artistic, athletic, or academic) creates the need for special custodial skills.

If the problem is central to the child's welfare, and if only one parent is qualified to cope with it, that parent receives favorable consideration. If, for example, a child is potential world-class tennis material and the father, the local tennis coach, works with her daily, the judge would favor him. Or if a child is dyslexic and the mother, a special education teacher, has been tutoring him, custody would probably go to her.

Custody Implications: Some instances, like those above, are clearcut, mainly because the special circumstances are not divorce-related; they preexisted the divorce and, in each case, let the parent establish a track record that speaks for itself as being in the child's best interests. When both parents or neither parent are specially qualified, these custodial skills lose their significance.

REQUESTING CUSTODY CHANGE: ITS HAZARDS AND HYSTERICS

You may think of custody modification as the wrap-up of a bitter divorce, a mere formality. Don't! Too many fathers are deluded, just as I was. They think the storm is past, that they can limp to a safe harbor, patch up their lives, and set sail for sparkling seas and azure skies. Don't let the typhoon catch you off guard.

The Price You Pay

I know there are fathers who sexually abuse their children, and I know there are Americans who sell security secrets to the enemy, and I respond with equal horror to both. It certainly never occurred to me that I would be the victim of a false implication of child abuse. Had the insinuation been true, I might have been equipped to deal with it. I might even have anticipated it; the guilty have the dubious advantage of knowing what to expect.

I'll never forget that September day. As I jumped out of bed, bright California sunshine streamed through the windows of my apartment, and fell like a blessing on the joy in my heart. After delays and postponements, the day I'd waited for had arrived. I ate breakfast with one eye on my plate and one eye on the clock, shoved the dishes in the sink, dashed through the shower, quickly donned the clothes I had selected the previous evening, and all but skipped out to my car.

Exactly a year before, the court had denied my request for shared custody. It classified my daughter as an infant because she was under four, and it favored maternal custody until that age, as many courts do. But now she had passed the four-year barrier. She was now a child, and the change from infant to child constituted a "change in circumstances," that many courts require before they will consider a request for visitation or custody change.

I would have preferred direct negotiation with my former spouse, but our current relationship precluded any possibility of a sane discussion on a subject she adamantly opposed.

So that sunny September day, my heart aglow, I was on my way to the Family Court Services Department for mediation, and I had every reason to hope they would grant me shared physical custody.

Everything was in my favor. Primarily, of course, the age change, but a lot more, too. Behavioral scientists and courts increasingly recommend shared physical custody because of its benefits to children. And I was well prepared. I had thought about, researched, and formulated a sound argument. Such were my thoughts as I pulled out of the driveway and glanced in the rearview mirror to make sure I looked okay. The first ill omen of the day stared back at me. I had forgotten to shave. Panic hit, created not by the blue shadow, but by the prescient flash of things about to go wrong.

I ran back to the apartment for a quick shave, and started for the courthouse again. The fraction of my mind not required to drive the car delighted in the days to come. At last, real time with my daughter. A camping trip to Yosemite. Three days in Disneyland. Long quiet companionable hours together. All just around the corner. No longer would I have to begrudge every tick of the clock, or resent the recurrent and perpetual return trips to her mother's that sliced off the visiting time until the commute seemed longer than the visit. No more picking my girl up and then, almost immediately, having to turn around and take her back. "Today will put all that behind me," I thought.

Never overly comfortable in the looming bulk of government buildings, I found the courthouse oppressive. The elevator inched its way to the sixth floor. I signed in and sat down to wait. My former spouse arrived late, accompanied by her boyfriend. This was a disconcerting development. Was he the chauffeur? I wondered. Or was he testifying in the mediation? And if so, what about? They signed in and left the area, evidently to avoid me. I tried to ignore the whole thing, reassuring myself that there is justice in the system and I was here today to collect some.

The child probation officer entered, greeted us, and directed us to his small office, leaving the boyfriend outside. (Apparently he was the chauffeur.) My former spouse and I, packed into the cramped office, sat facing the officer across the piled clutter of his desk.

I knew that I, as the person initiating the action, would be called upon first to state the nature of my request, and I was anxious to have it over with.

Through the one small window, I glimpsed the distant coastal range of mountains, which took me back to the meeting a year ago when joint custody was denied. At the conclusion of that meeting, the child probation officer had primly declared: "We do not grant joint physical custody to parents who cannot get along."

"But," I protested, "That's a Catch-22. If one party persists in being uncooperative, the other party can never get joint custody."

"That's not so," she snapped. "That's not the way it works at all." The lady contradicted herself. Should I mention that fact? I thought quickly. I know that the First Amendment guarantees me freedom of speech, a freedom of which I frequently avail myself. But I also know it doesn't guarantee that I won't have to take the consequences. The lady's indignation suggested to me, correctly or incorrectly, that the consequences might be a further loss of time with my daughter. I concluded that the risk was too high. I should just shut up. I did.

The probation officer's voice, asking that I present my request, reminded me that this was a different year, different circumstances, and a different court representative. I returned to the present with a sigh, hoping for better this year.

I presented my prepared statement, explained the reasons why joint physical custody would be in my daughter's best interests, and concluded with the argument that the state mandates the court to "encourage parents to share the rights and responsibilities of child rearing." Feeling comfortable with my presentation, I leaned back in my chair expecting agreement.

Far from agreeing with me, the probation officer informed me that, quite to the contrary, shared physical custody was not in the best interests of children, that there was "new evidence supporting this position." He had "read it in *Newsweek*." This meeting was going worse than last year's.

Child probation officers make high-level decisions, the results of which exert lifelong influences on the welfare of children. Most of them are trained professionals familiar, at a minimum, with their own professional journals and, in many cases, with major research projects in process, the results of which are not yet published. When this child probation officer quoted a broad-scope news weekly as if it were an authoritative narrow-focus professional journal, it was time to worry. And I did. If I couldn't expect professionalism, could I expect justice?

He then turned to my former spouse, who began by saying she was concerned because our daughter had begun to act strangely. She had taken to turning her dolls over and sticking things up their bottoms. Why, I wondered, had I not been told before? It was the first I had heard of it, and I had never witnessed any such behavior. Why was she bringing it up at this meeting?

A ploy, perhaps, to stop me from obtaining joint custody. Within the mediation structure, she was rebutting my argument by implying a concern about molestation. Without offering molestation as a direct objection to joint custody, without accusing me, without even mentioning my name she was, by implication, branding me a child molester. Essentially, the scenario boiled down to this. I asked, "May I have joint custody?" She objected. "I suspect child molestation." No one with good sense could have missed the tie-in.

Press reports of divorced fathers, falsely branded, flooded my mind. I saw those fathers, hundreds of them, deprived of their children's love, professions ruined, and alone. And I saw myself joining them. Numb, beyond fear and anger, in a melancholy akin to bereavement, I faced the possibility of never seeing my daughter again.

I could not believe I was listening to my former spouse making such a bizarre insinuation. I would not have been more stunned if the FBI accused me of selling classified military data. My mind, unable to establish any relationship between what was happening in the hearing room and what I knew to be the truth, retreated into a distorted Kafkaesque nightmare, groping about trying to find fragments of sense.

My former spouse continued, and I felt as if I were invisible and this conversation about my future with my daughter was being carried on around me. She had made an appointment with a child psychologist and the probation officer expressed approval of her choice, a fact I found far from reassuring, and ended the meeting saying we could go no further until we received the report.

There was first, disbelief; it wasn't real. The probation officer, standing up and pushing his chair back, seemed farther away, smaller. I tried to shake my head, clear my mind, but it didn't move more than half an inch in either direction. Shortly, everything returned to normal and with it came a chilling awareness that, while the insinuation was false, the threat was real.

Out in the sunshine again, numbness turned to rage. I refused to be a victim. I remembered the old Chinese proverb, "The journey of a thousand miles starts with a single step." My first step was to call my lawyer from the nearest gas station. She wasn't in, but after two hours of repeated calling I reached her and explained what had happened. I could feel the silence as she planned a strategy.

The second step, an appointment with the psychologist. I wanted to give her all the facts, not just a one-sided view. I wanted to explain my feelings. Let her see me. Let her see that I'm a normal concerned father, that I love my daughter and want what's best for her. I called, asked for an appointment, and told her I wanted to contribute background information about my daughter and my relationship with her and my relationship with my former spouse. I also told her I was supportive of her meeting with my daughter, and I wanted to do whatever was in my daughter's best interests.

The intervening three weeks dragged, dreary and tense. To me it was urgently important that this psychologist understand exactly what I wanted to say. But I feared that my concern, verging on desperation, was so intense I might blunder around and antagonize her, put her on the defensive or, worst of all, close her mind to me. I took notes, edited them, rewrote them, underlined them, all in my mind. My wife and I got away on a short vacation but, lovely as it was, the coming appointment overshadowed it. More than ever, at such times I am thankful for my wife's consistently perceptive understanding. Waiting was difficult; waiting alone would have been intolerable.

The morning of the appointment I was on edge, but the office was bright and reassuring, a desk on one side, a sandbox, toys, and two large dollhouses on the other. The psychologist was pleasant, direct, and professional, and we covered a lot of material in an hour. She gave me enough time to say everything I wanted to, and then explained what she intended to do. She would meet twice with my daughter, once with me and my daughter, and once with my former spouse and my daughter to see how we interacted with each other.

She said, pointing to the two dollhouses, that she would use a form of "play interview" to avoid the stress direct questioning would place on my daughter. She would have Taryn arrange the toy furniture to recreate two homes: one daddy's and one mommy's. Taryn would play out the activity in each home, and she would observe the activities to find out how the child viewed the homes and the people in them. She would then give Taryn two "anatomically correct" dolls to play with, and determine if any indication of abnormal behavior or sexual abuse existed.

There's an old Vermont saying: "You can't really appreciate the flowers of an East Coast spring unless you have lived through the snows of an East Coast winter." And you can't appreciate a real professional until you've been mangled by a few of the other kind. I left that office relieved, confident my daughter would be in competent professional hands.

Two weeks later my daughter and I met with the psychologist. We all sat on the floor, and the psychologist asked her to show me her toys. She was delighted to share her new creations with me, and I became an active participant in the fantasy world she had created. On my way out I spoke briefly with the psychologist. She lifted the whole world off my shoulders when she assured me everything appeared normal with my daughter. As confident as I was of the results, nothing could compare with hearing it from the psychologist.

After meeting with my daughter and former spouse, the psychologist met with my former spouse and me to give us her report and recommendations. She reported that Taryn evidenced separation stress commonly seen in children of divorce. It results, she said, from frequent transfers between the parents. Parents themselves, reluctant to part with the child, are stressed and the child picks it up and acts on it. She recommended that the child's stress be minimized, proposed a schedule that reduced the number of transfers by increasing the length of each visit, and doubled the number of Taryn's overnight visits with me.

I was, of course, delighted with the recommendation, and more than delighted that it came from the psychologist my former spouse had selected, and to whom she had brought my daughter, which I thought would make it more acceptable to her. When she refused to agree to the change, I was disappointed that she put her desire for more time with our child ahead of what, in the opinion of her own psychologist, was the child's best interest, especially in view of the fact that most of the time I was asking for would otherwise have been spent with a babysitter.

We both knew that the judge would accept the psychologist's recommendation and incorporate it in his court order. But not until I filed a motion with the court, got a court date, and she faced the time, money, and aggravation entailed in the court procedure, did she finally, one week before the court date, sign the change order.

Nine months after that sunny September day when I was so optimistic I had forgotten to shave, I walked out into the darkening evening and picked up the mail. I saw the attorney's envelope, ripped it open, and held in my hand a piece of paper that turned the psychologist's schedule into a matter of law.

I sat down on the curb next to the mailbox, oblivious of the light rain beginning to fall, and just stared into space. What a price to pay! But the reward — the opportunity to be the father I wanted to be, sharing in and contributing to my daughter's growth and happiness — the reward was priceless.

When I was thinking about writing this section of the book, I intended to omit anything relating to my former spouse's insinuations about child molestation. First, because it is painful and I preferred to forget it. Second, because it could reflect negatively on me. Innocence is not a sufficient protection. The charge of child molestation, once made, can stick forever no matter how false. When the media, the courts, or gossip publicly link a specific crime to a specific person, that person can be indelibly marked, and no evidence will eradicate it. People impulsively fall back on the old maxim, "Where there's smoke, there's fire."

My third reason for omitting the incident was that it could reflect negatively on my former spouse. There's no way to recount the incident without including her unfounded insinuations, and this could unintentionally portray her as irrational or villainous. I do not believe she is either. She is, I think, a victim of the current concern about children which we all share but which, even when grounded in fact, can escalate into hysterics.

Against my three reasons for excluding the incident, I had one reason for including it: I had conceived of this book as a way I could help other fathers avoid some of the agony I've endured. That objective placed upon me an obligation to be honest; it left me no room to shirk the presentation of useful material because of it's inherent unpleasantness. This one reason outweighed the other three.

Child pornography, child kidnapping, and child sexual abuse do most certainly exist, and we must protect children against them. Their prevalence, their monstrous nature, the vulnerability of children, the lifelong physical and psychological damage they can inflict — they all call out for nothing less than militant vigilance. Fathers and mothers everywhere respond to the call with search-and-destroy determination. And it is entirely commendable that they do so. But as America knows from experience, intense public fear and indignation can flame into a witch hunt. When every rope looks like a snake, the distinction between innocence and guilt blurs, and all are destroyed. The witch hunt endangers everyone, hunter and hunted alike.

We must first protect ourselves from becoming witch hunters. Most human beings are sensitive to group hysteria, but some are more easily seduced by it than others. Our own early history documents the guilt suffered by witch hunters who, at the moment of setting human torches afire, may have seen themselves as righteous administrators of justice. As I mentioned, I believe my former spouse acted in a form of witch-hunt hysteria. I state this, of course, as a personal opinion. As an adult, she is responsible for her own actions, regardless of her motivation.

We must, secondly, protect ourselves from becoming innocent victims of the witch hunter. Caesar, according to the Roman historian Plutarch, divorced his wife Pompeia because a wealthy young man, Publius Clodius, compromised her reputation by publicly pursuing her in spite of her objections. When asked why he divorced her when he knew she was innocent, Caesar replied, in a one-liner later popularized by Shakespeare, "Because Caesar's wife must be above suspicion." Two thousand years later and things haven't changed much. Should you ever — may the fates forbid — be blindsided as I was that awful day, lack of guilt will not protect you. You must also lack any appearance of guilt.

A subtle implication of guilt, such as I experienced, serves the same practical purpose as a direct claim. It delays any change in visitation until the investigation is complete, and it can take months, sometimes years. Up to this point, we've been dealing with damage inflicted by misguided, perhaps well-intentioned, former spouses. Now let us consider two additional and even more cogent reasons to avoid any appearance of guilt. First, for some parents the real goal is not custody. It is vengeance, retaliation for real or imagined wrongs. This person, one of nature's most deadly and volatile weapons, will zero in on any shred that can be twisted, rewoven, and colored as evidence.

Alayne Yates, M.D. writes: "When one parent accuses the other parent of molestation in the course of a custody dispute, this gains the immediate attention of the system. Law enforcement and social service agencies can swoop in, remove the child from a parent's home and forbid that parent further contact until an evaluation can be made. In the course of a custody dispute, when one parent initiates sexual abuse allegations which are later found to be false, the judge has sometimes denied that parent custody because the parent has misused the judicial system." [7]

This action is no loss to a parent who didn't want custody in the first place, whose singleminded aim was to get even with a former spouse, and it is of little satisfaction to the accused parent who, though not legally guilty, may live under the shadow of the accusation and never regain custody. The absolute propriety of your conduct becomes essential to your survival. Anything less, and you may lose your child and falsely carry the brand of child molester the rest of your life.

The second and most compelling reason for protecting yourself against molestation charges is that, by so doing, you also protect your child. Patricia Bresee, J.D., Geoffrey B. Stearns, J.D., Bruce H. Bess, Ph.D., and Leslie S. Packer, Ph.D. say that an allegation of sexual abuse is an indicator of emotional risk for the child, even in cases where the allegation is untrue. "Whether or not the allegations are true, the child is living in a disturbed parental environment. Either as the victim of sexual abuse or as the pawn of a malicious slander, the child is being misused or mistreated. The more hopeful possibility is that one parent is simply overreacting to evidence of possible molestation. Even this, however, may have caught the child in unresolved hostilities which are expressed through her and to her detriment. [8]

In addition, testing and observation of the child, which are essential to the investigation, create an atmosphere alien to anything the child has experienced, and with which she is ill-equipped to cope. Strange adults peer, poke, and question. Even when the charge is false, when there has been no molestation, when skilled professionals exert every effort to protect her sensibilities, the child, without comprehending the objective, is subjected to psychological and medical tests, discomfort, embarrassment, and invasion of privacy. The essential inquisitorial nature of the investigation, no matter how it is camouflaged, stresses the child. No effort is too great to protect your child from unnecessary investigations.

Of the 1.7 million child abuse cases reported in 1985, 65% (1,105,000) were unsubstantiated and, according to Dr. Alayne Yates, most false accusations arise in the course of custody or visitation disputes. [9] No one is exempt; the hazards apply to fathers of boys as well as to the fathers of girls.

At all times, but especially during custody disputes, you must be alert to anything in your conduct that could possibly be misconstrued. You may object that it violates your right to speak and act as you wish, and you may be right. If you were still living in the original family unit, such extreme discretion would be unnecessary. You can, however, with equal justification, make the same case against defensive driving tactics needed to survive our wild American freeways. You can challenge the system if you like, but you may reap what the wise old Greeks termed a Pyrrhic victory. A couple of thousand years ago, King Pyrrhus defeated the Romans, but the cost of the battle so far exceeded the rewards of the victory that he was sorry he ever got involved.

Society is peering at you from every direction. Many states require any child care custodian (teacher, licensed day care worker, foster parent, social worker), medical practitioner (physician, dentist, psychologist, nurse), nonmedical practitioner (public health employee, counselor, religious practitioner who treats children), or employee of a child protective agency (sheriff, probation officer, welfare department employee) to report any suspected case of abuse within thirty-six hours. Failure to comply can bring a misdemeanor charge punishable by six months in jail and/or a $1,000 fine.

Guard Against False Child Molestation Charges

Avoid being stereotyped as a "Father Abuser" and running the risk of inviting a false molestation charge. No single characteristic or combination of characteristics can reliably identify those fathers who molest their children or predict which fathers will molest their children. But molesters so frequently exhibit one or more of certain characteristics that there is a virtual stereotype. To say that a father fits the stereotype is certainly not to imply that he is a molester or even a potential molester. But a predominance of any of these characteristics can bring him under suspicion and increase the difficulty of defending himself against an unjust charge.

At some times, in some situations, all of us share some slight element of many of the characteristics. They do not stereotype us unless they are so dominant as to be extreme. If you find that you exhibit an unusually high degree of any of the following traits, a modification of your behavior could help you avoid a false molestation charge.

1. Alcoholism or drug dependence.

2. Inadequate impulse control. Physical violence. Temper tantrums. Inappropriate sexual conduct.

3. Emotional deprivation. Social isolation: immature or introverted personality; inability to make or retain adult friendships or social contacts; dependence on children for warmth and affection.

4. Rigid authoritarianism. Dictatorial control of every person, decision, and activity in the family unit.

5. Tendency to place a daughter in one of two extreme and diametrically opposed roles: "Daddy's Favorite," showering her with gifts and attention, and showing her excessive partiality over the other children; or "Mother and Homemaker," assigning her major responsibility for household or child care duties, and substituting her for an unresponsive, absent, sick, or deceased mother.

Using Open Communication to Avert a False Child Molestation Charge

Arden K. Weinberg, an attorney specializing in family law, says that open communication can ward off false child molestation charges. Secrecy, she says, fosters fear and hostility and leads to game playing, which in turn can lead to unfounded charges. The mother, trying to discover what the father is hiding from her, may seek answers from the child. This draws the child into the game, and puts her in a power position between the parents, giving her the ability to manipulate both parents and making her a potential pawn in a false abuse case. Good communication dispels secrecy. [10]

Attorney Weinberg advises: "Tell your former spouse more than she asks; give her more than grudging, minimal family information. Share with her on a continuing basis some of your child's experiences. Tell her, for example, that you went to the beach and that your daughter has a new dress. The more family event information you give your former spouse, the less her imagination is apt to run wild, the less your child is apt to convey slanted information, and the less apt you are to run into false charges." [11]

Erratic Behavior Can Signal Trouble Ahead

Erratic behavior or unexplained changes in attitude demonstrated by your spouse, can signal approaching trouble. Such actions do not necessarily identify the exact nature of the trouble to come, but they often signal the presence of resentment or hostility out of which trouble can arise. Behavior of the type listed below frequently presents itself prior to a trumped-up molestation charge. If you notice such behavior, be warned. Live defensively. Be circumspect at all times, and constantly examine your own actions for anything that might be misinterpreted and used against you.

1. Your former spouse suddenly begins to react erratically to visitations. She goes to great lengths to stop you from seeing your child. She makes you wait; has an excessive number of excuses for the delays; and forgets, or pretends to forget, her commitments to you about your visitations.

2. She clings to the past and refuses to go ahead with her own life.

3. She holds you responsible for her well-being, and blames you for every slight and misfortune she suffers.

4. Bresee et al. comment on behavior that is commonly attributed to mothers who accuse former spouses of child sexual abuse. "They are often accused of being overzealous, if not dishonest, in their efforts to keep their child away from her father. Some of these mothers who bring allegations of abuse display behavior that damages their credibility. They may be histrionic or combative and often aggressively demand that the decision makers act quickly against their ex-spouses." [12]

Be alert to any danger signals when you are involved in serious child or spousal support disputes. Stressful altercations can drive an otherwise rational person to making bizarre claims in an effort to gain the upper hand, and possibly to using these claims as blackmail to obtain financial advantage.

UNDERSTAND YOUR CHILD'S
DEVELOPMENTAL STAGES

The more you know about your field of work, the better job you can do, and the more you know about a child's developmental stages, the better parent you can be. A general knowledge of child development is important. If you don't know what to expect, you won't be able to identify the unexpected.

An understanding of physical development is not enough. You should also have some insight into mental and emotional development. Hospitals, colleges, and high schools offer a broad spectrum of theoretical and practical courses, evenings as well as daytime; libraries and bookstores provide a gold mine of material; newspapers and magazines bring you the latest research findings.

Sigmund Freud's work, especially his theories on early childhood sexuality, is an excellent starting point. It explains, for example, why a child shows affection to the parent of the opposite sex at certain stages, and how this affection, far from being devious or intentionally seductive, is a natural aspect of human development. It will help you see normal age-related behavior for what it is, a phase of development.

Sexuality, according to Freud, begins at birth, after which the human being progresses through several phases, during which, if he is to become a well-adapted member of his society, he learns to control his sexual impulses and achieve sexual fulfillment within society's rules.

Freud borrowed the name Oedipus from the Greek myth of King Oedipus, who, by unknowingly killing his father and marrying his mother, parallels a psychic activity common in three to five year old children, in which they wish for the death of the parent of the same sex in order that they may have complete possession of the parent of the opposite sex.

Contrary to popular belief, Freud did not formulate an "Electra Complex" applying exclusively to girls. The idea was suggested to him, but he rejected it. Instead, he applies the Oedipus complex to both boys and girls and, where sex makes a difference, he provides a specific explanation of the difference.

According to Freud, sometime before the end of the fifth year, the child's preference for the parent of the other sex reaches a climax. Then, after the end of the fifth year, the Oedipal period is followed by a lull that Freud terms the latency period, during which sexual progress is at a standstill and much is unlearned and undone. Following the latency period, puberty begins and sexual life resumes. Memories of the early period of sexuality fall victim to infantile amnesia which hides, from most people, events from birth up to the age of six or seven.

Freud says that, at puberty, ". . . when the sexual instinct first asserts its demands in full strength, the old, familiar incestuous objects are taken up again. . . ..The infantile object-choice was but a feeble venture in play, as it were, but it laid down the direction for the object-choice of puberty. At this time a very intense flow of feeling toward the Oedipus complex or in reaction to it comes into force; since their mental antecedents have become intolerable, however, these feelings must remain for the most part outside consciousness. From the time of puberty onward the human individual must devote himself to the great task of freeing himself from the parents; and only after this detachment is accomplished can he cease to be a child and so become a member of the social community. For a son, the task consists in releasing his libidinal desires from his mother, in order to employ them in the quest of an external love-object in reality; and in reconciling himself with his father if he has remained antagonistic to him or in freeing himself from his domination if, in the reaction to the infantile revolt, he has lapsed into subservience to him. These tasks are laid down for every man." [13]

According to Freud, it does little harm to a woman if she remains in her feminine Oedipus attitude. She will in that case choose her husband for his paternal characteristics and will be ready to recognize his authority. [14]

It would be silly of me to say that you can't be a good father unless you acquire some knowledge about normal child development. The evidence to the contrary is overwhelming. You can name a hundred wonderful parents who have raised great kids and wouldn't give a plugged nickel for theory. So can I. But understanding what's happening and what to expect enables you to catch and correct small problems before they become big problems, to take the responsibilities of fatherhood more easily, and make your relationship more comfortable for your child. A father's knowledge primarily benefits the child, but it is not without benefit to the father himself. Any father who is privileged to watch his child grow and change, and who doesn't make the effort to understand the complexity and beauty of the miracle taking place right under his eyes is, in my opinion, cheating himself.

WHEN A CHARGE IS MADE OR IMPLIED

When you approach a major freeway accident, you slow down, assess the situation, and proceed with extreme caution. True, your car is in top condition and you handle it like a pro on the open road. But until you pass the accident, you defend yourself against hazards; cars stopping short in front of you or slamming into you from behind, dazed victims suddenly appearing in front of your car, people darting out from between parked cars.

At the first sign of a false sexual abuse charge, slow down, assess the situation, and proceed with extreme caution. You face a more lethal hazard than an automobile accident. True, you're an innocent man, but it's not enough. Take immediate defensive action.

1. Remain calm.

2. Get your attorney's advice about the legal questions and what you should do right now to protect your rights.

3. List all the ways you can defend yourself. Always keep a clear,

total picture of your situation and the choices available to you. This list would include, for example, the "worst case" scenario if everything went against you, the possible restrictions relating to custody and visitation the court could impose, and the numerous defensive legal options open to you.

4. Beware of making panic decisions. Don't take a step without your attorney's approval. Don't sign anything until your attorney okays it.

5. Be especially wary of anything that sounds like plea bargaining. This is the court system's way of reducing the the number of cases coming to trial, and at the same time giving the district attorney's office a higher number of convictions. Everybody wins in this arrangement except you. If you are charged with a crime, the district attorney will try to negotiate some form of guilty plea from you. This plea will usually be to a lesser charge, or to a single charge on a multi-charge indictment. By making this guilty plea your sentence would be less than if you were found guilty at trial on the full charge. It sounds like an easy end to the problem but, like *nolo contendere*, it is considered by many people as tantamount to a confession, and can lead to further problems.

6. If a psychologist has been appointed, make an appointment so you can provide background information essential to a balanced understanding of the case.

7. Do not change your habits, your behavior, or your association with your child. Continue to see her and act exactly as you always do. Some fathers mistakenly think it is to the child's benefit to suspend contact until the charge is cleared up. But this can increase the child's stress. Your sudden absence may puzzle her and make her feel rejected at a time when she needs all the affirmation and support you can provide.

Secondarily, continuation of association with your child can, in itself, defend against the charge, even if the charge is made by the child. Doctor Yates says: "Signs which suggest that a child's allegations may not be accurate include . . . the child's continued, positive relationship with the person accused."

8. Your child is your child, not your confidant. Don't discuss your romantic involvements or your emotional problems with her. If you are driven by the loneliness of divorce and you feel you must talk to someone, find a sympathetic adult or join a single fathers' discussion group.

Don't burden your child. She is a child, not an adult, and she wants to be treated like a child.

9. For your child's benefit and for your own protection, know what you are doing before you attempt to provide sex education. In today's atmosphere, virtually everyone — teenagers, grandparents, men, women, employers, doctors, entertainers, teachers, and

divorced fathers — is vulnerable to false charges of sexual molestation. Most people whose official duties make them vulnerable to such charges take precautions to protect themselves. For example, doctors, whose personal and professional reputations are at stake, always have a medical assistant present at physical examinations of women.

10. Let the doctor take care of problems requiring examination or medication of the genital area.

Pick up some of the excellent "how to explain sex to a child" books available at your book store or library. They will help you understand your child's questions from her point of view, and provide simple answers appropriate to her age and understanding.

Use discretion. Keep your explanations and your language simple. Don't overload her with adult-type information that will only confuse her, and if you run into problems you feel you can't handle, get the advice of the child's doctor or psychologist.

11. Keep a detailed diary with emphasis on the time you and your child spend together. List where the two of you go, what you do, and the names of any other people involved in the activities. (Try to have other people with you when you are with your child. You may later want to substantiate your behavior, and a third party can increase your credibility.)

Add brief notes about your own activities and the names of your associates during the time you are away from your child, so you can reconstruct your actions should they be questioned by the court.

12. This section is addressed primarily to Children of the Age of Aquarius. But it won't harm anyone to read it. In essence, it was a beautiful age with its high spirits, its high aspirations, its pursuit of nature and simplicity. It was a time to discard the remnants of Victorian morality, reject straitjacket dress and behavior standards, encourage equality between the sexes, and affirm the brotherhood of all people.

Then, like all generations before us, having found our own identity, we put rebellion behind us, became proud and responsible parents, and joined the Establishment. But vestiges of our Age-of-Aquarius innocence left us ill-equipped to cope with society's bitter realities, one of the most bitter of which is the false charge of child molestation.

Naivete and a touch of stupidity lead us to believe that as long as we are innocent we will appear innocent. Doctor Yates tells about men who apparently learned the fallacy of this theory: "[One] case was based upon the man's photograph album which contained pictures of the little girl vacuuming the floor in the nude. . . . [in another case, a] young mother accused her ex-husband of molesting their four-year-old daughter only because he took showers with her during her summer-long visitation. On further questioning, she 'proved' he was a pervert because she knew he enjoyed reading *Playboy*. Another woman accused her ex-husband of molesting his six-year-old daughter because he was living in a homosexual relationship." [16]

Behavior can appear appropriate to one person and licentious to another, so we must conduct ourselves in a manner that discourages misinterpretation. Like IBM, the Army, and your local restaurant, society insists on its own dress code; comply, and you make life easier for yourself. Dress appropriately whenever you are with your child, especially if you are in the middle of a custody dispute, and especially if the child is a girl. Never bathe, shower, play, cuddle, or sleep in the nude with your child.

Protect your child from exposure to inappropriate adult discussions or activities, such as explicit adult films or photos, sexual activity, or parties where drugs or excessive alcohol are used.

Chapter 5

Finding the Right Lawyer

Justice has been described as a baby who has been subject to so many miscarriages as to cast reflections upon her virtue.

— William L. Prosser

This book is not about lawyers and legal technicalities; it's about miracles. But because the two frequently intertwine, an elementary knowledge of one is essential to the performance of the other. Your lawyer will explain the crucial things you need to know, at the time you need to know them. And your library can fill in background so you will grasp his ideas more quickly, saving his time (and his fees). But right now I want to alert you to some papers (summons and petitions), processes (defaults), and people (lawyers) that I see in your future. I wish I had known about them early on. I hope they soften the shocks for you.

THE SUMMONS

The summons, a short form, tersely and officially notifies you that a petition has been filed; identifies the parties, the court, and the case; and tells you (1) how many days you have to answer or appear, and (2) that if you fail to comply, you will be in default. (More about default below.)

Give the summons the respect it deserves. It's the opening bell, the gauntlet hurled at your feet. Your private disagreement has just exploded into a public spectacle.

A word about how the summons is served on (given to) you. A third party who is not involved in the divorce, frequently a uniformed law officer or a paid professional process server, hands you the paper. But it does not have to be given to you in person; other ways, such as publication in a newspaper, can satisfy the legal requirements.

When You Get a Summons, Get a Lawyer

The minute you find a summons in your hand, reach out your other hand, pick up the telephone, and find a lawyer. As soon as possible you need to spend forty-five minutes to an hour with a lawyer who has solid family law court knowledge and experience. He can analyze your situation, explain your options, warn you about hazards, and get you headed on the right path.

THE PETITION

Rarely does the first summons arrive alone. It is usually accompanied by a petition. It can be filed by the husband or wife, whomever initiates the divorce action.

It contains a request for divorce (dissolution), and the grounds on which the request is based. It also may contain a request for child custody, child and spousal support, and property division.

DEFAULT

Default as we use the word here means failure to appear in court (in person or through a lawyer) to defend or prosecute a case. It is to the court as failure to finish a contest is to sports; the difference is that the consequences of legal default are apt to be more profound.

Here's a simplified analysis of options; check with your lawyer about the complexities.

If you default, there's nothing further you have to do; you don't even have to appear in court. Your wife's petition will be uncontested, and the judge can grant all the requests contained in it, including such things as divorce, spousal and child support, and property division.

If you do not default, the court machinery processes the case through to the final decision. If you decide to answer, protect your rights by answering within the time the summons specifies.

To Default or Not to Default

Should you answer or default? Unless you have a grasp of the legal technicalities involved, don't try to decide on your own. Discuss it with the lawyer you consult; it is one of the most important reasons you should talk with him. Only you, with his guidance and based on the particulars of your situation, should decide.

In general, you will probably want to default only if there is nothing to decide. No money. No property. No children.

In any event, whatever you do, check with a lawyer first, and that brings us to the next thing I'd like to discuss.

LAWYERS

Lawyers have knowledge and experience most of us do not have. Even if we know the letter of the law, we lack the intimate knowledge that can be gained only through hands-on experience in the courts and with the rules and people controlling them. Shortly after receipt of the first court summons, most of us learn, if we were not already aware, that conducting our own legal affairs based on book learning is somewhat like piloting the Queen Mary II with a captain's manual in one hand. Enjoy the trip. Hire a captain, specify your destination, and keep an eye on the ship's progress.

Your lawyer knows not only how laws are written, but how they are interpreted. He is familiar with the court system, and knows how to deal effectively with its key people. He knows the forms required, the filing deadlines, and when and how these deadlines can be extended.

He can, therefore, analyze your position and formulate a plan of action, keep you aware of your options, assist you in making choices, and negotiate more objectively than your emotional involvement would permit. He can protect your emotional interests (child custody), your financial interests (home, car, business), and your wallet (alimony). He can save you from making stupid moves that his experience has taught him will not work.

Use a Short-Term Lawyer for a One-Time Consultation

You need a one-time consultation with a lawyer when:
- ▷ You first realize that your marriage is not working
- ▷ You first realize it is beyond repair
- ▷ The first time your wife is physically or emotionally abusive to you or your child
- ▷ When you and your wife first separate, regardless of whether it is you or your wife who moves out, even if neither of you is considering divorce
- ▷ When you receive the first legal papers.

Even if you know you have nothing your wife would fight for, an experienced divorce lawyer may know better. What about, for example, that Irish Sweepstakes ticket tucked in the secret compartment of your wallet? What if it pays off after the divorce? And what about that retirement pension you'll be collecting in a few years? Will it be mine, hers, or ours?

Just to make sure you know what you're doing and to fend off future problems, and for your peace of mind, a one-time consultation is worth the price.

Be mindful, however, of the old saying — any two lawyers can turn a peace conference into a battleground. Clearly, the more intense the battle, the more necessary the lawyer's services, the higher his fee will zoom. It follows then, that it is in a lawyer's interest, although unethical, to intensify the battle. Use your good sense. If there's nothing to fight over, don't fight.

You Need a Long-Term Lawyer to Represent You

You need to retain a lawyer to represent you and handle your case if a single issue remains unresolved: the divorce itself, property division, alimony, child custody, visitation, support, anything.

Short-Term: Find a Family Law Specialist

A one-time consultation is a short-term gap-filling measure. Don't waste time trying to get exactly the right person. Just make sure you get a reputable family law specialist.

If you have a business lawyer, he should be able to refer you to a good divorce lawyer for consultation. Or your friends may suggest some names. If you don't pick up a good referral quickly, call your local bar association; they will give you the names of several family law specialists. As a last resort, check the telephone Yellow Pages.

HOW TO FIND A LONG-TERM LAWYER TO REPRESENT YOU

If I could impress one idea on your mind, it would be that you need a lawyer knowledgeable about and experienced in family law, a family law specialist, who practices in the court where your case will be heard. Nothing short of this will do the job for you.

The family law specialist already has the book knowledge in his head; he works with it every day. (Get anyone else and you'll pay for his time while he searches through law books to figure out what form to file next and how to file it.)

The family law specialist already knows his way around the family law court; he knows the personality and the bias of each judge, and he knows which of them will probably be philosophically sympathetic to your position, increasing your possibility of a fair deal. (Get anyone else and you'll pay for his time while he checks the opinions of his friends in family law, or else you'll take your chances on his flip-of-a-coin selection.)

Check Out the Sources

Check with recently divorced co-workers, friends, and acquaintances. Be wary of the lawyer whose client thinks he got a great deal. It can indicate an unfair settlement, and possibly that the other party was taken advantage of by a lawyer who wins by any means, regardless of who suffers. An unfair settlement in your favor sounds great; it's not what you want. It won't be your former wife who suffers, it will be your child. Unfair settlements create deep-seated resentment and antagonism, shadowing every aspect of your truce with your former wife and, through her, your association with your child. All you want is a fair and even break.

Ask about the lawyer's knowledge, experience, industry, reliability, and accessibility. Judge not by the cash he can save you, but by how well and fairly he can represent you.

The local bar association will give you a list of family practice lawyers. Don't mistake it for a Good Housekeeping Seal of Approval. It's not selective as to quality; it is a list of lawyers who have registered themselves as being available for this line of work. I do not intend any negative implication about the lawyers on the list. I just want to tell you that you should do your own checking.

About Friends, Relatives, Neighbors, and Sex

Think carefully before retaining a friend, relative, or neighbor as your legal advisor. Even if he doesn't charge, it is usually inappropriate and inadvisable to hire someone so close to you.

A lawyer's professional loyalty must be finely balanced. Diverse facets are pledged to you, his client; to the court, of which he is an officer; and to the ethics of his profession. Toss in another element, personal loyalty to you (as distinguished from professional loyalty), and the result can be awkward and painful to both you and the lawyer.

It can increase the stress of discussions about expenses, charges, payments, time delays, tactics, and accessibility. It can make negative decisions more painful for both of you. And it can almost rule out the objective and impartial representation you need.

The question arises: Is it better to hire a male or female lawyer? I've heard a lot of interesting arguments, but I doubt that the question can be answered in the abstract.

I think it's safe to say don't hire a chauvinist of either sex. The male may turn your case into an "us against them" effort rather than working for a fair and reasonable decision. The female, on the other hand, may just as easily turn it into a "win one for the women" tournament. Other than that, it appears to me that the sex of your lawyer is irrelevant. Some people are more comfortable working with people of one sex or the other. And that's fine, too.

Let me add that my lawyer was a woman. I selected her not because she was a woman, but because she was the best damn family law specialist I could find.

THE LAWYER TO AVOID

Stay far away from the lawyer who:

▷ Has impressively grand offices and a high lifestyle; someone has to pay for them.

▷ Tells you everything you want to hear. This is frequently the same one who, later, will tell you everything you don't want to hear when he explains the judge's decision.

▷ Has the loudest mouth and the quickest answers (including, as you'll discover, why it didn't come out the way he predicted).

▷ Guarantees results. The outcome of a court case, like the outcome of a horse race, cannot be guaranteed. A lawyer who does so is kidding you or kidding himself; either way, he's dangerous.

▷ When you ask a reasonable question, says: "Trust me."

THE LAWYER TO LOOK FOR

Be prepared to put your trust in the lawyer who:

▷ Is sympathetic to your philosophy of shared parenting.

▷ Can give knowledge, support, and direction.

▷ Believes in, and will work for, your cause.

▷ Is a tough, skilled, and ethical negotiator.

▷ Tells you what you need to know.

▷ Gives his straightforward opinion of your position, the courses of actions available, the probable outcome of each, which he recommends, and why.

THE INITIAL INTERVIEW

Most lawyers want to talk to you about your case because they want to do the job and collect the money. That's fair. They have to pay their bills, too. When you call, explain that you would like a brief non-advisory meeting; that you do not want legal advice at this time;

and that your purpose is to get a sense of whether the two of you could work together comfortably.

Personally, I think that a lawyer should not charge for an initial non-advisory meeting during which he provides information about himself so you can decide whether to hire him. When he interviews prospective employees, I would be surprised if he reimburses them for the interview time.

Ask if he charges for the meeting and if so, how much, and will it be applied to your account if you engage his services. Some lawyers don't charge, some lawyers charge and apply it to your account if you subsequently hire them, and some lawyers just charge. Find out which and how much.

In this connection, I would like to pass on a tip given to me by a New York cabbie. I jumped in his cab, which happened to be un-metered, and gave him the address. When we arrived and I stood by his cab, digging the fare out of my wallet, he craned his neck down and looked up through his window. "Ya' look like a nice guy," he said "so I'm gonna give ya some advice. Ask how much before ya get in a cab what ain't got a meter. Stand on the curb, ya get a fair price. Sit in the cab, the price goes up. We know we gotcha."

A lawyer's office, like life, is an unmetered cab. Stay on the curb until you get a fair price. Otherwise, they know they gotcha.

Ask the Right Questions

Ask about his background:
> ▷ What is your academic background?
> ▷ How long have you been in practice?
> ▷ What is your experience in mediation?
> ▷ Roughly how many divorce cases have you handled? What type? And the outcome?
> ▷ What is your normal procedure in a divorce case?
> ▷ Under what conditions do you take a case to court?
> ▷ How many of your cases go to trial?

Ask about your case:
Tell him your goals and ask his opinion of their attainability.
> ▷ What is your opinion of current divorce and custody laws? And of shared custody and responsibility after divorce?
> ▷ Will you handle my case personally? Will you hand it over to a junior associate? If so, what area or areas, and how closely will you personally monitor it?
> ▷ Will I meet with you or someone else?
> ▷ How much access will I have to you or others?

Ask about his fees in detail:
> ▷ Will you require a retainer?

▷ What is your payment schedule?

▷ How much do you estimate my divorce will cost?

▷ How do your hourly and your flat rates run?

▷ Approximately how much would a flat rate be for my case? Roughly how many hours?

Each rate has its disadvantage. The hourly rate sometimes runs up the time, increasing the fees. And the flat rate can decrease the time, sometimes below the minimum required.

WHAT TO DO AFTER YOU HIRE A LAWYER

Tell Her Everything

You can be certain that what you don't tell your lawyer, your wife will tell her lawyer. And when her lawyer reveals the facts, your lawyer will be unprepared and unarmed. And there goes your case.

The confidentiality of anything you say to your lawyer, unless it involves the commission of a crime, is protected by law. Tell her everything, things that are painful to discuss, things you'd rather forget, things that you are ashamed of. You can be absolutely sure she's heard worse. Hiding the truth, glossing it over, telling half-truths or untruths, or altering the facts will work against your case.

This is the time for the truth, the whole truth, and nothing but the truth. When she learns about it in court from your wife's lawyer it will be too late. Cooperate.

Don't hire a person and then make it difficult for her to do the job. That's biting off your nose to spite your handkerchief.

Keep appointments and be on time. Follow through on what you tell her you will do. If for any reason, you don't intend to follow her advice on a specific matter, let her know. Otherwise, you will be going in one direction, she will be going in another, and your wife's attorney will be delighted.

Respect her time; don't call every time you argue with your former wife. When you do telephone or meet with her, make a list and have it in front of you so you can communicate your questions quickly and completely. Don't waste her time or her staff's time; you are the one who will pay for it eventually. Think before you lift the telephone.

Keep Records

Don't be caught with your memory down. Keep an accurate and detailed diary of events. Include everything and anything that can possibly bear on the case including legal events (receipt of papers, hearings, meetings with anyone remotely concerned with the case);

names, places, dates, times; planned or chance meetings and conversations with your former wife, members of her family, or mutual acquaintances; time spent with your child. Nothing compares with precise and thorough records for giving you credibility, in or out of court.

Keep copies of documents, and a document is anything in writing pertaining to the situation: letters, memos, telephone messages, notes on the back of envelopes or menus. Again, anything.

Keep a diary of all charges and consultations, in person or by phone, with your lawyer. This is especially helpful in clearing up honest disagreements about charges.

Know what your lawyer is doing on your case. Make sure she is working in your best interests, and that she is giving your cause the time it needs. No hardworking well-intentioned lawyer, and most lawyers are, will resent your concern. Keep an eye open for laziness (like failure to return urgent calls or meet important deadlines) and sleaziness (like incurring unnecessary expenses by requesting information through deposition that is being volunteered without deposition).

Appreciate Your Lawyer's Efforts

Be grateful that your lawyer does what you pay her to do. Don't expect her to comfort you and listen to your personal woes and grievances. That's not her line of work. Take it up with a behavioral science major.

If you are fortunate enough, as I am, to have a dedicated and effective lawyer, give her your trust and your cooperation. It's a tough, adversarial, scrappy world she works in. Don't make it worse.

IF YOU CHOOSE THE WRONG LAWYER

Most of us, driven by work or personal inclination, have at some time moved from one city to another. Routinely, just as we found a new place to live, we found a new doctor, so we are familiar with the waivers and transfer of files involved. Lawyers, unlike doctors, are not an everyday necessity in most families, but the mechanics of getting a second opinion or changing lawyers are similar.

For those with the good sense or good luck to have avoided legal altercations, let's briefly look at getting a second opinion.

Go back to your original list of prospective lawyers. Assuming that your present lawyer was number one on that list, call number two.

Tell him that you are uneasy about the way your lawyer is handling your case, and would like a second opinion. (Find out what his hourly rate is.) Most lawyers will be glad to hear from you, but some don't like to get caught between lawyer and client, in which case continue on down the list.

Before the appointment, write down your questions to make sure you cover everything, and to save his time and your fee. Odds are he will reassure you that your present lawyer is doing a good job. If, however, he confirms your fears, don't be afraid to change lawyers.

Make arrangements to have this, or another, lawyer handle your case.

Notify your original lawyer that you intend to transfer. She will require a written statement providing the name and address of the new lawyer, and authorization to transfer the file to him. Your new lawyer will then ask her to send him the file, and he will notify all parties concerned of the change.

A second opinion is not a major project, and when it is needed, it pays for itself in peace of mind. But changing lawyers is expensive, and it should not be undertaken frivolously.

You remember when you hired the original lawyer? All the time and money? You'll have to go through all that again. Plus he will have to familiarize himself with your file, which means another bill for his time and another delay. And a change of lawyers does not guarantee you better representation.

Don't even consider a change unless your present lawyer has given you reason to distrust her judgment, her integrity, her industry, or her effectiveness; is not giving your case the attention or getting the results she indicated she would; or is not properly protecting your interests.

If you consult a doctor about chest pains, and he slams you in the hospital for a triple heart bypass with what seems to be inadequate tests, you don't have to be a medical doctor to know you've got a doctor problem.

When your lawyer gives you the legal equivalent, you won't have to be a lawyer to know you've got a lawyer problem.

HOW TO SAVE YOURSELF SOME LEGAL FEES

You can do a lot of your own work and cut your legal fees if: you have been exposed to legal and court procedures, are essentially realistic, are willing to learn more and work hard, can clearly define and state what you want, if you have the guidance of a good lawyer, and if you can keep your head when those about you are losing theirs.

Not all lawyers will let you participate because it changes their function from representing you to advising you, leaving them vulnerable to liability problems. Some who do go along with the idea require you to sign a document acknowledging your position.

I was fortunate in having a lawyer who permitted me to do some work, with her guidance on questions of law, procedures, and legal exposure. This way I frequently bypassed the negotiation network, that awkward system through which you speak to your attorney, who speaks to your former wife's attorney, who speaks to your former wife, gets an answer from your former wife, and starts it back to you through channels. While sometimes necessary, it is neither efficient nor accurate. Its inherent tendency to distort both the content and the tone of the communication can transform a request into a demand, angering everyone and creating friction and resistance.

I cut four message relay steps, two people, and substantial expense by negotiating with my former spouse's lawyer in her law office. I did not sign anything until I had studied it carefully and my lawyer had reviewed it.

It also keeps you in the middle of the action. You know what's going on; you don't have to sit and bite your fingernails wondering why your lawyer doesn't call back.

Chapter 6

Making a Home for Yourself and Your Child

A house is a home when it shelters the body
and comforts the soul.

— Phillip Moffitt

TO MOVE, OR NOT TO MOVE, TO A NEW AREA

Remaining in the old area makes life easier for everyone, including your child. The closer (but not close enough to revive hostilities with your former wife) the better. Close proximity can: maintain an unbroken flow of familiar ties, friends, schools, shops, medical and recreational facilities, the continuity of which will help your child tolerate the physical and emotional disruptions of the divorce; make both parents available in an emergency.

Moving out of the area (although it can sever destructive emotional ties to your former wife) will present short-term and long-term problems.

Among the possible short-term problems are checking out the safety of a new area — traffic, robberies, mugging, child molestation, narcotics, gangs. This will require you to read local papers and talk with local authorities. (Should you move any distance, an excellent resource that most people overlook is your auto and homeowner's insurance agent. His business is risk insurance; it requires him to know what's going on and he, unlike the authorities, has no vested interest in keeping it under wraps.) You may have to find a whole new network of services for yourself and your child.

Long-term problems, each of which is time-consuming and exhausting, present themselves later. The greater the distance, the more complex the problems, but among them are establishing emergency arrangements to handle serious problems in your absence, working out the logistics of getting the child back and forth to school, and scheduling and arranging transfer and travel between the two homes.

Prepare Your Child for the Move

Change, good or bad, is unsettling. But your child will feel a lot easier if you prepare him ahead of time. Don't make it sound like family visiting day at the county jail. ("I'll be living all alone by myself in a strange new place. I don't want to leave, and I'll miss you. It will be lonesome, but maybe you can come visit me once in a while.")

Be upbeat, enthusiastic: "Now you'll have not one but two homes. You'll have your own space and we'll decide together where to put your toys." And tell him some of the interesting projects you are planning for the two of you. Above all, be enthusiastic. A child will take his attitude and his tone from you. If you sound as though it's going to be a drag, it will be a drag for him; if you sound as though it's going to be an adventure, it will be an adventure.

Watch for Danger Signals

Change brings stress, and stress can bring problems. Most children will exhibit mild episodes of the following symptoms in the course of normal development; that is to be expected. When they become a pervasive pattern, however, they may be danger signals.

PHYSICAL — Any unusually marked tendencies toward the following: nail biting, nausea, sudden weight gain or loss, stuttering, hyperactivity or lack of energy, bedwetting, excessive or inadequate sleep, violence, tantrums, tics, chronic fatigue, hostility, aggression.

EMOTIONAL — Significant and/or uncharacteristic: excessive desire to please adults, rebellion, sleep disturbances, nightmares, sleepwalking, depression, secretiveness, anger.

CHANGE — Drastic and sustained change in attitude toward family members, friends, peers, teachers. Decreased interest in schoolwork or school activities, hobbies, sports, clothes and general appearance. Lowered achievement i.e., lower grades, difficulty in concentrating, inattention, tardiness, truancy. Or, conversely, a desperate need to overachieve.

HOME, COMMUNITY, POLICE — Danger signals include running away from home, uncharacteristic problems with neighbors or storekeepers, vandalism, stealing, cult or gang membership, use of liquor or drugs.

Too Few Symptoms, Too Many Causes

It's fairly easy to spot most symptoms; in fact, it's hard to escape many of them. You and I would most likely notice immediately that a child has run away from home or taken to liquor or drugs.

The challenge is finding the cause of the child's symptom, and it is complicated by the fact that the human stock of causes is larger than its supply of symptoms. Consequently, one symptom (crying, for example) can stand for many causes (loneliness, guilt, stress, hunger, sleepiness). On the job we run into the adult version of this problem, for instance, when we know the boss is angry about something, but we don't know what. We see the symptom without being able to find an exact cause, so we turn to a friend and ask something like: "What (cause) is the boss angry (symptom) about today?"

Some Time-Tested Ways to Get at the Cause

You may already have the answer in the back of your head. From the advantage of adult perspective, you may have sensed a developing problem without having brought it into full consciousness. Search back for anything unusual, anything that might warrant the child's response.

The child himself is an obvious possibility. It can't hurt to ask.

"What's the matter, Champ?"

"Joey and Tommy won't let me play with them."

"That's great. Now you'll have time to play with me. Been looking all over for you to play a game of checkers. Let's get the board out, shall we?"

If direct questioning fails, I have a game that reverses our roles so my daughter can talk about what's on her mind without talking about herself. I propose that we make believe I am very, very unhappy, and she has to guess what I'm unhappy about. I play it up melodramatically while she does a child's version of brainstorming, and sometimes we open up a clogged communication channel.

Don't press the child too hard. A simple problem can grow so large in a young mind that it becomes like an impacted tooth. Unskilled poking will make it worse.

Brothers, sisters, or friends may be aware of the problem, but finding out requires sensitivity, tact, and a knowledge of the children's network. If there's any risk of their taunting him because his "Daddy wants to know what the crybaby is crying about," don't do it.

Anything beyond these elementary levels requires a child psychologist or psychiatrist. And if you ever doubt the value of getting professional assistance when you need it, read Michael Reagan's heartbreaking account of being molested when he was very young, of his inability to tell his parents about it, and of the resulting years of guilt, pain, and alienation from his mother and father.

WHEN YOU MOVE

Safety First!

Walk around the neighborhood with your child. Help him discover hazards such as dangerous traffic spots, mean dogs, and dark or unfrequented points where thugs could loiter unnoticed. Talk with him about ways to avoid them.

Help him find the best and safest routes to places he will go by himself — stores, libraries, friends' homes, school. If a local parents group has set up "safe houses," point them out so he will know where he can go if trouble arises.

Scout the garage and yard for potential hazards to your child and his friends. Trim overgrown hedges and bushes to eliminate hiding spots that could invite suspicious characters to lurk about. Clean out rubble, broken glass, sharp objects. Discard old refrigerators and batteries. Replace or repair rickety treehouses, swings, athletic equipment, bicycles, toys. Install a child-proof secure cover over or a fence around the swimming pool (should you be so lucky as to have one come with the house).

In the house or apartment itself bring security up to standard, including door and window frames and locks. Eliminate safety and fire hazards, and check to see that all fire alarms are in good operating condition. Most police and fire departments will make no-charge safety and fire inspections. Determine the best fire escape routes, and run a few drills with your child so he'll know what to do if he faces the real thing one day.

Detergents, disinfectants, garden supplies, cleaning fluids, alcoholic beverages, medicines, gasoline, paint, guns — keep them all out of reach of children (especially of very young children) and, if possible, under lock and key.

Check for toxic plants (oleander, castor bean, azalea), fauna (scorpions, certain spiders and snakes, and bees and wasps, especially in hives subject to being disturbed by children).

Don't leave appliance cords hanging from counters or shelves within reach of children. The same goes for cords on window blinds.

Purchase a well stocked first aid kit. Place it in an easily accessible location and let everyone know how to use it.

Constant, alert supervision is the only real assurance of safety (barring earthquakes or other natural disasters) for small children. It's okay to blink now and then, but do it rapidly.

MAKING YOUR HOUSE A HOME

Your new house is not a hotel, it is not a summer camp, it is not a place your child visits. It is your home and your child's home. Keep this thought in front of you as you allocate space and select furniture, and you can't go wrong.

Most of us, at this point, are financially unable to duplicate our former homes, nor should we try; we can easily forgo some of our previous conveniences and luxuries. If your child misses something specific, say the swimming pool, get him a bigger swimming pool — take him to the beach or the local YMCA. Ingenuity, imagination, and enthusiasm can be as effective as dollars.

Give Your Child a Voice in Fixing Up the House

The two homes need not be alike nor look alike. To make the child's transition less stressful, however, they should function alike. They should lend themselves to similar activity patterns, so he can easily transfer his learning to this new home. For example, if everyday silverware was in the lefthand drawer, put it in the lefthand drawer here. If extra rolls of bathroom tissue were under the sink, put them under the sink here. This way he'll soon feel as at home in his new home as you do on your job. But if he has to learn new patterns, he'll feel as strange as you did your first day on the job.

Encourage your child to help you select the furniture and decide where to place it. Taking a hand, however small, in the shaping of the house will help him settle in and feel that it really is his home.

I would suggest something akin to the trendy, but misnamed, Japanese Participative Management, the main advantage of which appears to be that it gives everyone an opportunity to express his opinion fully while retaining final control in management's hands.

Of course as your child gets older, you can move toward a junior partnership, and delegate the decisions you feel he can handle.

Personalize Your Child's Room

First, scale the child's room to his size. Bed, desk, chairs, tables — all should be size and age appropriate. Clothes hangers and shelves should be within his reach.

Toy chests should be free of locks or latches that could trap him inside. They should be large, simple, and safe, preferably in light plastic so the lid, should it fall, will not injure his head or fingers. If you already have a heavy chest you plan to use, examine it for child-proof safety, especially the locking device that holds the lid up. If it fails the safety test, use it elsewhere, and get a safe chest for his room.

Sufficient and accessible storage space for clothes and toys installed at this point, will simplify discipline. Without it, the child will suffer the frustration of trying to do a job without proper tools.

Give him a free hand in decorating his room. The goal is to make it his room, not to win a design award. Here, unlike the living room, anything he wants is okay. Tiger pawprints all over the drapes and bed, he says? Tiger pawprints it is. If he wants to hang a big cardboard nameplate on his door, that's okay, too.

Bring special toys, records, and clothes from his other home. This will emphasize continuity.

Create the same personalization in other areas that are primarily for his use for, let's say, homework, music, or reading.

Observe the Privacy of His Room

Every person, including a very young person, needs a private place of his own, a place where he can be alone, sense his individuality, and think his own thoughts — where he can quietly evolve into the person he is becoming. As most divorced fathers know, a private area is sometimes out of reach. That's okay. A corner of a quiet room, blocked off by standing screens (a sort of indoor tent) will serve, just so the area is his, is private, and others do not enter uninvited.

MAKING YOUR VISITING SCHEDULE WORK

A precise, mutually accepted schedule carried out with goodwill on both sides can forestall problems and decrease hostility.

When a court grants visiting and custody rights, it issues a formal court order that, like our Constitution, speaks in general terms. The schedule, an informal agreement between you and your former wife, details the specifics by which the two of you will carry out the court order. Earlier we discussed the importance of establishing visiting and custody rights at the beginning of the separation. Without rights, there can be no reliable schedule. So we'll assume you've already taken care of the rights, and move on to the schedule.

Set up an initial schedule quickly. Don't dally over minor decisions. You can renegotiate later.

Make Special Days Really Special

Share holidays fairly. Alternate so your child can spend Christmas at one home this year and at the other home the following year, and do the same with birthdays and holidays.

When your child is with you for the "Big Days," make them really big. Get into the spirit and celebrate in a big way. If children's parties lie outside your area of expertise, pick up a couple of books at your bookstore or library. They make it easy to set up simple, colorful, inexpensive parties that children love.

Successful Scheduling Demands Realism

The key question you must answer before you can even talk rationally about a schedule, is exactly how much of each twenty-four hours is already preempted by other activities.

Most of us have two distinct types of commitments. We easily identify the first because it is time-specific. We know precisely when it begins and when it ends — work, school, clubs, committee meetings, associations.

But we tend to think of the second as optional because it is time-flexible. The fact that we can set the hours seduces us into thinking we don't really have to do it. We dismiss the reality of these hours, much as we dismiss the reality of the dental chair — until we have a definite appointment. This floating-hour category includes after-hours work-associated correspondence, reports, parties, conferences, workshops, and informal socializing. If you are taking any additional school or professional courses, this time classification also includes study, assignments, group projects, field trips, and teacher conferences. And, of course, as yet unscheduled traffic schools and dental appointments.

You cannot be in two places at the same time, an immutable law of human existence. Ignore it and you will inevitably subject your child to disappointment and rejection which, in time, will become indifference. Expecting your arrival, she will be greeted instead by your excuses. She will, like most of us when we are cancelled, look first to herself as the cause. In time, however, she will see that the failure is yours. She will become inured to disappointment and callous about your cancellation. (A friend of mine puts it this way, "You can't hurt me because any place you kick me I have a callus.")

Carefully tote up all your time-specific and time-flexible commitments, and sign up for no more hours than you actually have.

Successful Scheduling Focuses on the Child

Most child psychologists say and most parents agree that while children may thoroughly enjoy both homes, much of their pleasure is destroyed by the partings at the beginning and the end of each visit. As adults we know the sadness of parting from those we love. The child feels, in addition, a responsibility for making one of the parents unhappy by leaving, which induces a sense of personal disloyalty and guilt that complicates and intensifies his sadness.

Schedule as few short visits as possible. Longer visits, because they require fewer partings, decrease the likelihood of your child developing the separation stress frequently seen in children of divorce.

No matter how young your child is, listen to her preferences, but keep control of the scheduling. Don't allow her capricious whims to dictate arrangements. It will inconvenience everyone and benefit no one.

As the child grows older, her preferences will merit added weight, and the schedule at that time should be adjusted to accommodate her school, sports, and social activities and, eventually, work.

Successful Scheduling Demands Cooperation

In preparing the schedule, you and your former wife will no doubt disagree on such points as the precise time a particular visit begins and ends, and the place you are to pick the child up and return her. Disagreements of this nature, positioning you on different sides of the battle line, can easily deadlock the schedule.

Try to avoid deadlocks. If it's something you can change without serious disruption to your own life, do so. If there's no way you can make the adjustment, negotiate. You gain nothing by insisting on your way just to get your way. Cooperate whenever possible, and in doing so have an understanding that you expect the same cooperation when you need it. Lose a little time this week, you may need a favor next week.

Handle Transfers With Care

Almost any meeting with your former wife is a demilitarized zone strewn with wartime land mines. But in my experience, pick up and return of your child are the grandest high-tension events of them all. As you pick the child up, your former wife parts with her. As you part with her, she regains her. For every happiness and sadness you experience, she experiences the reverse, and for every happiness and sadness she experiences, you experience the reverse.

Leaving your child after a visit is the saddest, but picking her up at her mother's house is the most nervewracking. You are torn between the happy expectancy of time with your child and the apprehension of an encounter with your former spouse. The child's mother is torn between the sadness of parting with her child and resentment toward you for taking her. The child is torn between wanting to be with you, wanting to stay with her mother, and the guilt she feels for her mother's unhappiness. The tension of and between her parents communicates itself to her, increasing her own stress.

One particular day sticks in my mind. For weeks I had looked forward to seeing Taryn. Then the day arrived, and my stomach, on schedule, began to tie itself into fancy knots. What would I meet at the door? Questions? Financial demands? What new gem? What new surprise?

"If only my daughter (then a toddler)," I thought to myself, "could drive!" I smiled as I thought that's just the kind of absurd solution my brain supplies when it has thrown up its-hands about finding a functional answer. But the concept, no matter how whimsical, that I did not have to drive, gave rise to three workable solutions: 1) Set up a neutral place (a park or shopping mall). It would minimize the child's sense of leaving home and deserting her mother. 2) Pick the child up at, and return her to, her school or day care center. 3) Have an uninvolved third party, acceptable to both parents, pick the child up and return her.

Prepare for the Visit

Prepare. Make plans, no matter how simple. Arrive enthusiastic, with a head full of ideas, looking forward to a great visit. Get the day off to an exciting start.

Visits need not be all play and no work. Include everyday responsibility and discipline. Your child will develop a healthier sense of reality. It's unfair to the child and to his mother to indulge him to the extent that his two homes present an unrealistic contrast.

Not all visits will work as planned. Some will require change. Others will entail disappointment. You can turn even that kind of day to use. Take the opportunity to discuss the fact that life doesn't always work out as planned. Children can't learn that too early.

Call before the appointed time if you will be late or if you will be unable to keep the appointment. Explain why you will not be there in terms that the child will understand. Cancellations feel like rejections unless they are convincingly explained.

Beginning the Visit

The goal is to have a happy visit with your child. Keep that in mind, and everything else becomes trivial.

Be on time. Limit your conversation with the child's mother to the subject of the child and the visit, such as confirmation of the time of return, or that you will pick up the gift for the birthday party your child is going to. Rehashing the problems of your former marriage and other such irrelevancies is inappropriate.

Let me alert you to an inherent "pickup" problem. If it hasn't happened to you already, it will.

Your child may suddenly decide, to the accompaniment of tantrums and stamping feet, that she doesn't want to go with you. It's a bad scene. You will feel overwhelming pain and rejection, but it will, most probably, have nothing to do with you personally. Maybe the child is sick and just doesn't want to go anywhere with anyone. Or she may be responding to the emotional stress of the situation. Or she could have had her heart set on playing with friends next door. Or a dozen other reasons.

Don't react emotionally. Think in terms of your child, not yourself. The first priority is obviously to determine if the child is sick. Ruling this out, get the party on the road as quickly and as quietly as you can. Until a child is, at a minimum, twelve years old, it is wise to keep to the schedule. If she willfully tears down the protective restrictions that surround, she will not only feel a threatening loss of security, but she will be encouraged to get her way by manipulation.

Concluding the Visit

If you have agreed to feed the child during the visit, don't bring her back hungry. Inform the child's mother of any important observations, changes, or problems. Don't loiter. Kiss your child goodbye and tell her when you'll see her again.

GETTING ORGANIZED ON A
TWENTY-FOUR HOUR DAY BUDGET

To be a good parent, make time to enjoy your children, take care of business, live your own life. All this in twenty-four hours a day? Yes!

Keep the "In" Box Empty and the "Out" Box Full

When I was twenty-two years old, I worked briefly in an office whose manager was the tops. The first morning he must have seen that the job terrorized me, because he sauntered over, dropped into the chair beside my desk, smiled, and quietly said, "I know this job looks real mean, but actually it isn't. All you have to do is take the papers out of the in box, do something with them, and put them in the out box. Keep the in box empty and the out box full, and you'll do just fine."

What a wonderful manager! What wonderful advice! His words have stayed with me, and they have simplified my life. Whenever I hit a snag, I start removing things from the in box, literally or figuratively. It starts me rolling and I'm in high gear before I know it.

That's all there is to organization. Know what to do next, and keep moving.

Make Lists: Your Lists are Your In Boxes

Every ten minutes you free up is another ten minutes to spend with your child. Lists will help; you won't waste time trying to figure out what to do next.

Each member of the family, especially you, should prepare and maintain a set of lists using the procedures we discussed earlier. Each set should contain three lists: 1) Do today. 2) Priority. 3) Non-priority. You will find the headings broad enough to encompass all projects, and sufficiently explanatory to insure that the right projects land on the right lists.

Chip away at the "Today" list first thing. Do errands early, you'll save time. Traffic is lighter, shops are less crowded, and salespeople are less harried.

Be flexible. Know what you're going to do next, but be willing to switch jobs in the interest of efficiency.

For a real timesaver, include your simple projects in child-centered time. Children enjoy "helping dad fix things." It's also instructional. Try these group projects: wash the car, fix a leaky faucet, sweep the garage, paint the fence, weed, water, or plant the garden, run errands.

The more your child is an active participant in your home life, rather than an onlooker or visitor, the happier you both will be.

Chapter 7

Your Parenting Style

Ingenuity, plus courage, plus work, equals miracles.
— Bob Richards

PREPARING YOUR CHILD TO COPE
WITH THE LARGER WORLD

To a child, the world outside her home — with all its traffic and toy stores and restaurants — exists only as a dazzling, unfathomable outer space into which she occasionally ventures, much as an astronaut braves the moon. Her family group is her real world, a small, personal world in which her parents plan, organize, administer, and control the circumstances of her life. One day she will live in that larger world.

Preparing her to live there comfortably, confidently, and wisely is a primary responsibility of parenthood, as binding on a divorced father, while the child is in his custody, as on a father of an intact family. Your parenting style will be a major influence on your child's preparation, or lack of preparation, to cope with the outer world.

THREE PARENTING STYLES

Parental authority, like business authority, is expressed in three basic managerial styles: autocratic, indulgent, and situational. These styles do not exit in airtight compartments. Occasionally the autocratic parent lapses into indulgence, for example, or the situational parent turns autocratic, but each style retains its dominant character despite an occasional breach here and there.

Once upon a time, parents, like managers, used to unconsciously fall into one of these three styles. But expanding study of managerial styles now lets us consciously select the style we want. Here's a quick look at the three choices.

Autocratic Style Parenting

This style focuses on today. The parent makes all decisions, issues orders, inspects results, reprimands failures, and awards very few medals. He seldom talks and never listens.

ENFORCEMENT: The parent's power rests on the child's dependency and resultant fear of mental, emotional, financial, or physical punishment.

ADVANTAGES: It gets the job done efficiently and quickly, teaches the child to obey orders, and protects him from making mistakes.

DISADVANTAGES: It teaches him how to follow orders rather than find answers, and it deprives him of growth and decision-making experiences.

EFFECTS: To look for a standard result from any parenting style would be to make the simplistic assumption that, for each stimulus, only one response is possible. We deal here with so many variables that, until we have considerably more research, probabilities are all we can hope for.

With the autocratic parenting style, submissive children can become highly dependent on leaders, comfortable only when they have precise directions and regimentation; for them, life in a straitjacket can come to represent security. Independent children on the other hand, frequently learn to do as they are told, repress resentment, and plan their escape.

Indulgent Style Parenting

This style, too, focuses on today. But this parent agrees with everyone and disapproves of nothing. He laughs and plays and fixes things that go wrong, and pursues popularity with the single-mindedness of a political office seeker. He always smiles and never says no.

ENFORCEMENT: The parent, fearing the loss of the child's love, abdicates all authority and the balance of power drops, by default, into the child's hands.

ADVANTAGES: It exposes the child to a broad range of experiences and eliminates parent-child conflicts.

DISADVANTAGES: It turns the child loose in a wilderness of experience with no guidelines and offers decision-making opportunities, but isolates the child from the consequences of her choices.

EFFECTS: The child sees the world as a place where others will solve her problems and answer for her actions. Then, as an adult, she is thrown on her own to fend for herself, lacking adequate knowledge, experience, or discipline.

Many of these children never grow up; they remain forever irresponsible, immature, and dependent. The survivors, and undeniably there are a considerable number of these, too, fall back on their own values, temperament, and character, and develop their own capabilities and resources. But I couldn't sleep if I were to willfully submit my child to such jeopardy.

Situational Style Parenting

Like Aristotle's Golden Mean, this style lies midway between the excesses of the autocratic and indulgent styles, and I admit to being strongly biased in its favor. Only parents who take a situational approach can, in my opinion, create miracles in a child's life, miracles of happiness, growth, and self-actualization.

This style focuses on today and tomorrow. Its keynote is flexibility. The parent considers each situation individually, analyzes it, determines the best interests (current and future) of the child, and responds accordingly, calling on autocratic discipline in crisis, and on indulgent love in times of non-hazardous play. The parent communicates clearly and openly. He frequently smiles, sometimes frowns; often says yes and sometimes says no.

ENFORCEMENT: The parent's authority rests on a parentchild bond of mutual love and respect. The child's power derives from her inalienable human rights.

ADVANTAGES: This style teaches the child to interpret and react rationally to the outside world, and provides a semi-protected environment in which she can experience the consequences of increasingly high levels of decision-making.

DISADVANTAGES: It is time consuming, demanding, and requires constant flexibility.

In a world without guarantees, this style appears to be our best bet for preparing a child to live a full, happy, productive, and ethical life. Most children who are raised by situational parents make an easy transition to the larger world outside the home. Many, if not most, become self-confident, self-reliant, and self-directed adults.

How to be an Autocratic Father

Complete instructions are available in any military manual dealing with how to command troops, so I won't take up your time with them here.

How to be an Indulgent Father

When your child asks anything, just say "Yes."

How to be a Situational Father

The purpose of this book is to tell you everything I have learned about situational parenting, and you'll find detailed information throughout. But let me set out a brief overview here.

Establish a warm, approving, supportive, and loving relationship with your child. Establish a mutually open fear-free two-way communication. Be aware of her needs. Stay tuned to her feelings. Listen to her wishes. Be patient. Don't compare her ability with yours, compare it with your ability at her age.

Be flexible. Keep everything possible open to negotiation. Do not require perfection. Give her responsibility and place emphasis on learning, progress, and improvement. Acknowledge and praise every new accomplishment. Encourage her interests. Teach her to do things for herself.

Never lose your belief in miracles, your sense of wonder, or your sense of humor.

Chapter 8

Communication

God gave us two ears and only one mouth so
we can listen twice as much as we talk.

— Zeno of Citium

EVERYDAY MIRACLES OF COMMUNICATION

A jet roars overhead. A rose blooms. The telephone rings. The sun sets. Natural and man-crafted miracles stream through our lives, unnoticed and unexamined. We accept them as we do the fact that we eat when we're hungry and sleep when we're tired. That's the way things are.

The act of communicating with other human beings is one of the most used, and least examined, of our everyday miracles. But unlike most common miracles, communication requires constant attention; left to itself, it plays tricks on the speaker and the listener.

Let me give you a personal example. Some months ago, I stopped at the bank to cash a $100 check. I didn't want a lot of small bills so I said to the teller, "May I have $20 bills, please." As I watched in surprise, she counted out twenty one-dollar bills. Several possibilities raced through my mind: She didn't hear me. She did hear me, but her boss is watching and she wants to look busy. She has nothing but dollar bills. She's tired of people telling her what to do, so she's going to do it her way.

Then it struck me. I understood why she was counting out all those ones, and it was my fault. I had not communicated my idea. I had mentally pictured $20 bills. But she, not seeing the $ sign inside my head, misinterpreted my request, and, with every justification, responded to what she heard and gave me twenty one-dollar bills.

I learned from that experience. If ever I have occasion to repeat the request, I'll rephrase it, "May I have five twenty dollar bills, please."

THE PROCESS OF COMMUNICATION

Life boils over with demands on our mental and physical energies. We grab priorities off the top of the pile and run with them. Rarely do we have time to look at the whole social, economic, and political structure. We're lucky we get time to play our part, let alone explore behind the stage scenery.

Look, for example, at how we think of flying to London. 1) Get a ticket. 2) Board the airplane. 3) Sit for hours. 4) Arrive at Heathrow. 5) Deplane. 6) London. No time to contemplate the overall process that makes the flight possible. And no reason to. It's in competent hands; bringing it into our awareness would add nothing.

We see communication in the same simplistic way: 1) I said. 2) He said. Underlying this superficial view of communication is the presumption that an idea can be transmitted, easily and without alteration, direct from one mind to another. From this false premise, we arrive at the equally false conclusion that when I (speaker) make a statement, you (listener) hear and understand exactly what I mean.

The difference between a London flight and communication is that we can get to London without knowing how it's done, but we cannot communicate effectively unless we have at least a basic understanding of the mechanics.

Every communication, even the most elementary, results from an intricate process of generation, encoding, sending, receiving, decoding, response, and feedback. And despite constant effort, an idea is rarely understood exactly as sent. But ruling out parapsychology as, at best, unpredictable, communication is our surest bet, so let's take a look at how it works and how to make it work for us.

We are primarily concerned, at the moment, with talking with our children, so we will focus on oral communication, as opposed to written communication, although the two have much in common.

> ▷ **Generating:** My first step in any communication is to decide what I want to say to you.

> ▷ **Coding:** Once I am clear about that, I have to put it in a form I can send through the air. First I must transform my thought into signals (language).

> ▷ **Sending:** When my idea is coded into language, it's still not quite ready to send. I still have to turn the language into sound waves that vibrate the air. The process is much like the telegram seen in old western movies. The telegrapher could not send the piece of paper through the air, so he coded its message, and tapped out the code on his machine which sent the message over the wire in the form of electric impulses.

I now complete the coding of my message to you by transforming the language into sound waves which I can send into the air between us.

▷ **Receiving:** When the sound waves strike your eardrums they are transmitted to the hair cells of your ear's cochlea where they are turned into nerve activity. This nerve energy signals your brain, which processes the signals and perceives the sound waves.

▷ **Decoding:** Still another step is required. Your brain interprets the sound waves by reversing the coding process discussed above until it figures out the message or an approximation of it.

▷ **Response:** You don't have to respond at all, of course, but if you do, you become the sender, and I become the receiver, and you take the generating, coding, and sending steps above.

▷ **Feedback:** Let's say my message to you is: "May I take your car?" You can respond verbally by saying, "No." Or you can respond physically by handing me your keys. (You have innumerable alternative responses, including hysterical laughter at the idea of anyone letting me take a car, but we'll keep it simple.) Either way you verify that you received and decoded my intended message with fair accuracy, just as the actions of the bank teller fed back to me the information that my message had misfired.

My message to you can be wiped out at any of the steps above. Far from shooting right into your brain, it treads an intricate path, threatened at every twist and turn by internal and external forces, subject to distortion, misinterpretation, and obliteration. Nothing can guarantee its undamaged arrival, but awareness of the process and care in its execution will raise the odds.

COMMUNICATING WITH YOUR CHILD

When Your Child Talks

Be available. Don't discourage the child with "Don't bother me now, I'm busy." or "Another problem! Can't I have a minute to myself?" Assure him you want to talk with him. "I'd love to talk with you right now, but I can't. I've got to finish this report." Then tell him when you can talk, "This should take about another half hour. How about if we get together then?"

Pay attention. Don't let your mind drift off to golf, taxes, or the roof that needs fixing. Show that you are interested.

Listen actively. When he tells you something important, such as, say, being embarrassed by a teacher, recognize its importance. Rephrase it and repeat it back to him, so he will know you heard, acknowledge his feelings and, if possible, suggest a way to avoid a recurrence. "I understand. You must have been embarrassed when the teacher corrected you in front of the whole class. It must have been painful. Maybe you and I should work a little harder on that kind of problem so you'll have it down pat next time."

Ask questions that will help him elaborate the idea or story he's telling you.

Encourage him to express his feelings and his moods, joy, delight, playfulness, wonder, anger, fear, outrage, pain.

Don't censor subjects because they make you uncomfortable. If you ignore unpleasant feelings and pretend they don't exist or act as though they should not be discussed, they will not go away. They will go underground. Your child may give up trying to talk with you, deny his feelings, and develop an unreal sense of his emotions.

Listen to everything he tells you. It's the only way to find out what is on his mind, and there's no shortcut. Listening to him, carefully and respectfully, is also the best way to teach him to listen to you, even when he disagrees with you.

Validate his feelings. Give him feedback to tell him you heard and you understand. "You must have been surprised when the whole class sang 'Happy Birthday to You.'" . . . "I'm glad they found out it wasn't a real bomb, but I'll bet was frightening at first." . . . "You were very brave when you fell and twisted your knee. I'm sure it was painful."

Don't change the subject. Let him finish what he wants to say.

Don't jump to conclusions and answer his questions before he completes them.

"Hey, dad, can I . . ."

"No! I've told you a dozen times you can't go to the movies this afternoon. Now don't ask me again."

You're not dealing with an adult who has the sophistication to slam back at you, "Hey, how about letting me finish my question before you answer it?"

You bring your child to an abrupt standstill, part of his question still hanging in his mind, and an answer in his ears that doesn't fit the question. You'll never know what his question was. And after a while he'll give up asking you about anything. No point in consulting a deaf oracle.

If he angers you, take a few minutes to calm down. Silence can sometimes communicate effectively.

When You Talk

Look directly at your child when you speak to him. Observe his facial expressions. If you lose his attention, find out why. If his eyes glaze and his head slowly bobs and drops toward his chest, he didn't get enough sleep last night, or he's sick, or you talked so long you overshot his attention span, or your repetition of complaints is boring him. If he looks puzzled or confused, ask why. Did you say something that wasn't clear? Or something that puzzled him? Something he disagrees with, maybe?

Sarcasm has no place, at any time, in your conversation with your child for two reasons. First, it doesn't work. He'll remember the hurt and forget what you told him. Second, he'll pick up the technique himself, and one day you'll wonder why you don't get respect.

Separate the child from the act, and talk about them separately. All of us seek the security of being loved for ourselves, for what we are, not for what we do. Young children especially need the security of continuous and unchanging love.

Avoid statements like "You are a bad boy for doing that." When you say the child is bad, you condemn him as a person, make him fearful of losing your love, and block his ability to communicate freely. Open communication requires voluntary vulnerability, and this involves the risk of alienating the listener. Fearful children cannot take such a risk.

Better to say, "I love you, but what you did was bad." This statement condemns the act, not the child, and brings reform within his grasp. He can't change himself into a different person. He can change his actions.

Apply the same rule to positive words. Separate the child from the act. When your child puts his toys away, don't say: "What a good boy you are for putting your toys away." To a child, "You are a good boy" is the same as saying "I love you." When you add "for putting your toys away," you say that your love depends on what he does. It follows that he can lose your love by doing or saying something wrong, and fear inhibits the free flow of communication.

Better to recognize the action without commenting on the boy: "I see you picked up your toys. Your room looks really great."

Don't label your child. Adjectives applied to him may become part of the way he sees himself, and we all tend to act in accordance with our mental pictures of ourselves. If "stupid," "dumb," "clumsy," or "mean," become part of his self-image, he may well live up to it.

Thank your child for coming to you. Tell him you appreciate his having enough confidence in you to talk openly, and that you will always be there to listen and help.

Be a showman, end on a light note. Show people know how to

turn a mediocre act into a happy memory, "Leave 'em laughing!" If the subject is too heavy for humor, at least leave him on a positive note. "You and I will work on it, and I'm sure we can fix it." "I'll call the school and see if we can change the schedule."

COMMUNICATING WITH THE ENTIRE FAMILY

The Objectives of the Family Communication Meeting

▷ To give each family member a voice in family affairs.
▷ To facilitate achievement of family goals, enable the family to operate as an organized unit, rather than a random collection of individuals.
▷ To plan and coordinate family activities and encourage cooperation and team work.
▷ To provide a forum for open discussion, negotiation, and resolution of family problems, complaints, conflicts, and grievances in a non-crisis setting; improve communication within the family; and keep all members informed of events affecting the group.
▷ To prepare children for leadership, and provide a working model of democratic government in action in which they can acquire negotiation, compromise, and communication skills and a knowledge of organizational procedures. To teach children to take responsibility for their decisions and their actions.

How to Schedule the Meeting

The meeting should be a routine part of family activities, once a week, on the same day, at the same time, and when everyone's available and distractions are at a minimum.

For most families Sunday morning or Sunday evening works out best. Unlike other days, Sunday signals the beginning of a new week; this is an ideal time to review the past week and plan for the coming week.

The time should be adequate to conduct business, not more than one hour, and each meeting should begin and end at the designated time. If meetings are too long, they are boring; if they are too short, they are ineffective. It's the chairman's job to move the meeting along, keeping it lively and on time (more about this below).

Emergency Meetings

A weekly meeting guarantees each decision a minimum seven-day trial before it can be voted out, unless an emergency meeting is called. When you change the schedule, you take a risk that a good idea will be voted out without a fair chance. In addition, too many emergency meetings rob them of their special character. They should be called as infrequently as possible, and then only with the unanimous approval of all voting members.

How to Stage a Meeting

Your family meeting is primarily a business conference, and should be staged like one. It should be held around a table, any table, dining room, kitchen, or a couple of planks on sawhorses. People sitting upright, facing each other across a table, are ready to pay attention, think, and participate. A businesslike setting brings out the adult in the youngest family members.

Levels of Decision Making

Some decisions are made by adults, and are binding on all members of the family. Some decisions are made by vote, and they, too, are binding on all members of the family. Each voting member has one vote, and all votes carry equal weight.

A unanimous vote is necessary to pass any decision. The advantages of this requirement outweigh the disadvantage of its cumbersomeness. It eliminates the danger of a small minority being outnumbered and becoming resentful and obstructive. If all agree on an action, they are more apt to comply with it. Reaching consensus provides valuable experience in compromise and negotiation.

Forums will provide opportunity for full and open discussion of a subject by all voting members. They will have no voting authority, and the conclusion reached will have no binding power on the membership, unless they are later voted upon.

Who Should Attend

Voting members include all members of the family whose lives and activities are affected by decisions made in the meetings: mother, father, children, as well as anyone living as a member of the family: grandparents, aunts, uncles.

Non-voting guests includes friends and visitors — anyone connected with the family but unaffected by its decisions. Other guests might be parents who are contemplating a family meeting and would like to see one in action, and occasionally, close friends of the children.

Invitations should not be extended lightly. The presence of outsiders can favorably or unfavorably affect the meeting. Contact with people from outside the circle broadens children's social experience and competence, and an outsider's interest can heighten awareness of the meeting's purpose and importance. On the other hand, the presence of guests can inhibit and distort free discussion. Selection of guests requires sensitive matching of the guests and the children involved.

Officers of the Meeting

Each meeting requires a chairman. He's the traffic cop. He opens and closes the meeting, keeps it on schedule so everyone can speak and all necessary business can be completed, and he controls its activity including the subjects considered, and when the members speak and when they vote.

The father should conduct the first three meetings, so everyone can see and think about how it is done. After that, it should become a revolving chairmanship, transferring to a different member, in turn, at each meeting. Early experience of this key function will be of lifelong business, social, and political value to a child.

If a child has adequate language skills, but is not quite up to the total job, you might consider sitting with him as a consultant. I belonged to an organization whose president had difficulty with Robert's Rules of Order. He simply appointed one of the members who was a lawyer to sit with him at the head table and advise him about fine points of order. It worked out great. We kept an effective president and our meetings kept their legitimacy.

Every meeting also requires a secretary. He's the record keeper. At each meeting, he records attendance, activity, and decisions. At the following meeting, he reads his report and, after he makes corrections and the group approves the report, he maintains it as part of the family's permanent records.

Establish a Positive Atmosphere

Everyone should actively participate in discussions and help resolve conflicts.

Everyone must comply with the rules of the meeting. No person is to speak until he is recognized by the chairman, and when a person is speaking, the other members must remain silent and listen. No member is to bring up certain subjects which are off limits, such as problems with his mother.

Everyone must demonstrate respect and good manners, and help others feel comfortable and free to express their views. Sarcasm, nagging, name calling, and tantrums are out of order. Members must not be criticized, during the meeting or later, for not attending.

How to Structure a Meeting

The following general meeting outline will get you through initial meetings, but I am sure that you will want to check your bookstore or library for a simple handbook of meeting procedures so you can refine the techniques as you go along. Later on, nothing will get your child such immediate and positive notice as the ability to chair a meeting with competence and assurance. Now is the right time to get him started on the correct procedure.

The chairman calls the meeting to order, welcomes the group, and thanks them for attending.

The secretary reads the minutes of the previous meeting. After corrections and changes are made and approved, the report is accepted by the membership and becomes a part of the group's permanent records.

OLD BUSINESS: Discussion of business not completed at the previous meeting or old issues reopened.

NEW BUSINESS: Announcements and discussion of new plans, finances, complaints, grievances.

RECOGNITION: Positive time to publicly praise progress, improvement, and achievements — anything from hanging up clothes and keeping shoes in a straight line, to practicing the piano or winning a college scholarship.

I'm going to take a few minutes here to discuss the importance of recognition time. I think recognition may be the meeting's most important function. It is to the family what the annual awards banquet is to the corporation. And it should be structured like a corporation banquet.

1) To retain audience interest, begin with the least significant accomplishment and climb the ladder to the most spectacular achievement. If you start with the big items, the audience yawns at anything less. They've walked in on the car-chasing, crashing, final scenes of a film. They've seen it all. Why hang around to see the beginning?

2) But this is neither clear cut nor especially easy to grasp: To get full value out of recognition, a leader must consciously focus forward as well as backward. He must publicly praise in the individual the behavior he wants in the group.

When a run-of-the-mill leader recognizes an individual's achievements in the presence of a group, he is primarily concerned with closing the account by publicly paying the individual his due. A good leader realizes that he is also providing positive reinforcement that will encourage the individual to repeat the achievement. But only the most sophisticated leader understands the full importance of public recognition.

The sophisticated leader leaves nothing to chance. He knows he is shaping the future behavior of those listening. In a masterly show-and-tell demonstration, he appeals to man's common hunger for group approval (shows the individual held up to public applause) and explains how others can do it (tells how this individual did it). Now everyone in the group knows how it must feel to be a rhinestone cowboy, and how he, too, can have all the lights shining on him.

You, too, can save yourself a lot of hassle and effort by using the desirable behavior of each individual as a foundation from which to shape the behavior of all.

MEETING REVIEW: Brief, clear summarization of the meeting's major points.

Everyone loves a happy ending. Plan a special dessert, an outing, a sing-along, games, joke-telling time.

Repetition dulls the brightest activity, as children are quick to inform us: "Do we have to sing again today?" Vary the nature and duration, and keep it secret. Everyone will look forward to the next meeting.

THE MIRACLE OF LONG DISTANCE CLOSENESS

Vary the Message and the Media

Distance, even such that precludes weekend, even monthly, visits, need not prevent you from maintaining a close and loving personal relationship with your child, as warm and real as if you were living next door.

WRITE LETTERS AND CARDS — Write letters varying size and content — anything from a short note ("Just to say I love you, and I'm thinking about you," or "I heard a great joke today, and I thought you'd like it.") to a multi-page comment (about something he said, did, or wrote — or an account of something you've done) that might interest him.

Keep a supply of pre-addressed envelopes, stamps, and pens handy so you won't have to poke through several drawers for the equipment. You'll write more and enjoy it more.

Send cards. Holiday cards are a cheerful way to be with your child in spirit, especially on child-centered holidays — Christmas, Valentine's Day, Easter, Halloween, and any others of personal significance to him. Get the card in his hands no later than the day itself. A card that drags in late says that it was prompted by a sense of duty rather than love. You didn't care enough to take pains to get it there on time.

Scenic postcards of places you plan to visit together and those you have already visited together, with appropriate personal messages, give added reality to his home with you and his future with you.

Never, ever let his birthday accidentally slide by without a card from you.

Add special sparkle to a special occasion: send a telegram. I'll bet it will be the first telegram of his young life and he'll be delighted. A telegram surprises all but the most jaded of adults; it will surprise your child even more.

TELEPHONE — Before you telephone your child, keep a list of what you want to tell him, such as funny or interesting incidents at work and people who asked for him, especially people his age.

Keep his visiting schedule near the telephone, so you can remind him that you will be seeing each other in only (number of days) from now. Mention any new information you have on your plans for his next visit. It will promote anticipation and increase his enjoyment of the visit, but keep your ears open. If anticipation turns into impatience or anxiety, downplay the visit for a while.

Make arrangements, by mail or during a phone conversation, about when you will call him next. It will give him a specific time expectancy and a sense of certainty. Make the call when you said you would, not a day later, not a week later.

If anything prevents your meeting the schedule, get word to him ahead of time, including an explanation and, if possible, set up a time when you will be in touch.

Make calls interesting and reasonably brief: Keep a running list of questions you want to ask about school, sports, homework, his friends, movies he's seen.

Don't ask questions he can answer Yes, No, or okay,. e.g., "How's school?"

Answer: "Okay."

You didn't learn anything you didn't already know. You might just as well not have asked. Besides, it shows no interest in him as a person. Kids know that adults who don't like kids ask questions like that and never listen to the answers. It's almost as bad as forgetting his name.

Do ask questions that can't be answered in one word, that pertain to him specifically, and that indicate you remember what he tells you, e.g., "Tell me about your science class demonstration Thursday."

Let him answer that in one word.

Listen for details and follow them up. Like, "How did you finally decide to reproduce the visuals?"

PHOTOGRAPHS — Pick up a camera and a supply of film. Have a friend snap you on the job, watching TV, playing soccer, cooking, riding a bicycle, gardening, or doing things in which he is specifically interested. Write a personal note on the back of each shot.

Encourage him to send pictures of himself and his friends. Ask specifically for his school photographs. Comment, in writing or on the telephone, about each photo you receive, and individualize the comments. "You look like a champ on your new ice skates," will mean more to him than "It was a nice picture."

Mention what you do with the pictures: "I'm beginning a photo album of your pictures." "I framed the shot of you on the school bus, and I keep it on my desk in the office. I'm really proud when people say what a handsome young man you are." "I carry your class photo in my wallet."

Steel yourself against receiving pictures of him with his mother, or his mother with other men. They may not exactly brighten up your day, but they are part of his life and if you want to know what's going on with him, you have to take the bad with the good.

If the cost of sending pictures is somewhat steep for him to handle, you might want to buy him a camera, supply the film, and pick up the developing and mailing costs.

AUDIO AND VIDEOTAPES AND GAMES — Send him audio or videotapes of your activities, around the house, at work, driving, doing the dishes, attending ball games, golfing — anything that will keep him in touch with your everyday life. You could ask a friend to make a tape of his arrival at the airport and at the house, and send him a copy. Encourage him to plan and create tapes of his friends and activities and send them to you.

Play games like chess or checkers over the telephone or by mail, or collect coins or stamps together.

To make it easier for him, provide stamped self-addressed padded envelopes of the type used to protect tapes so he can just drop them in the mail to you.

Ask him to send school newspapers, reports, and projects. If he sends you drawings, you can send him photos of them hanging on the wall.

Subscribe to a local newspaper in his city, so you can stay current with the events and sports he's interested in.

GIFTS — Gifts can be a splendid and tangible way to say "I love you." They can tell your child that he's always in your heart and you will be always there for him. If, and I emphasize the word if, you use discretion, they can keep you in his heart, a real and central part of his life, regardless of distance.

If you try to play a year-round Santa Claus, gifts can assume an importance of their own that blocks you out. Response to their arrival can shift from "A present from dad!" to "A present from dad."

I remember, for example, a classmate whose parents regularly sent him cash. He became so addicted to the money itself that he would hastily tear off one end of the envelope, shake it to see if any money fell out, and toss it aside to read when he had nothing else to do.

To this day, the memory revives the same forlorn sense of pathos it engendered in my school days. I still have a mental picture of parents writing faithfully, deluded into thinking that their letters were eagerly anticipated. They were forgotten. The money had become the message. Reserve the Santa act for Christmas Eve.

RULE OF THUMB: Big Gifts are for Big Days. Little Gifts are for Everyday. Nothing wrong with spectacular gifts, if you can afford them, on his birthday and Christmas. The remainder of the year takes more ingenuity; the trick is to vary the size, character, and value of gifts so their arrival never stales. Send him a magazine subscription on his field of interest, an unusual shell picked up on a beach where the two of you spent a day, a small mechanical toy you happened to notice, film for his camera, tapes for his recorder, a record, a stamp or coin for his collection, a poster of his favorite rock star.

CONSIDER COMPUTER COMMUNICATION — Don't mention a computer to your child until you talk it through with his mother. You might not reach agreement, in which case you would have to withdraw your offer and disappoint him.

The price of computers is tumbling every day. But there's a lot more than the original price involved. Add to that the continuing and not insignificant cost of peripherals, programs, games, computer furniture, pricey paper, ribbon cassettes, additional disks, specialized instruction books, and in fairness to your former wife (unless she herself is a computer whiz), a service and maintenance contract. Save yourself future headaches; settle on how much it will cost, and who's going to pay what.

If you work things out, you can set up a terrific communication channel by linking your two computers together through the telephone system. It will also (and this might be a selling point with the child's mother) give him an early and painless headstart in computers, a knowledge of which is becoming increasingly essential every day to success in school and business.

Chapter 9

Family Activities

*It would be better if they told their children, "Go out
and play in traffic."*

— Tazewell Banks M.D., Cardiologist, Washington D.C. General
Hospital, concerning parents who allow their children to eat
foods rich in saturated fats at fast food restaurants.

FOOD IS A FAMILY AFFAIR

Food and group membership are essential to man's survival. Lacking food a baby will die in infancy; lacking group membership, he may survive physically, but without human interaction he will never develop into a human being. Throughout history — from prehistoric hunters gathered around the fire to an American family gathered around the Thanksgiving table — man, recognizing the importance of food and group membership, has celebrated them in the communal meal.

The contemporary family, or at least the modern American family, is gradually losing touch with the significance and the experience of the communal meal, and with its going, each family member is losing touch with the roots of his essential humanity.

Let's not wait for Thanksgiving to restore the communal meal to its central position in the family. Let's make every day a celebration of family warmth, love, laughter, and unifying human interaction.

Get the Family Together

As individuals, we have become so accustomed to eating when we feel like it that we have come to think of it as a provision of the Bill of Rights. Getting everyone together at one time may require serious negotiation and compromise.

A family communication meeting is the ideal forum for discussions of this ilk. I would, however, warn against casually throwing it on the table. Without proper preparation and persuasion, it will be voted down. I suggest that a member of the family, one who is enthusiastic about the idea, take it on as a project, as though he were a senator trying to get a bill through Congress. He could research it, anticipate and prepare to meet the objections, and present it at a family meeting.

Make the Meal Magic

Disconnect the telephone. Turn the message machine on, and turn the television off. Turn the radio or stereo on, low, for background music only. (If the younger members don't revolt, play classical records or tune in a classical music station; it's an excellent opportunity to indoctrinate their ears.)

Everyone should dress appropriately (especially nice on big occasions).

Everyone should demonstrate good manners, not only in eating, but to everyone at the table and in personal conduct. A book of manners beside the cookbook facilitates good manners. Not, for heavens sake, one of the old-fashioned stuffy books. Pick up one of the modern publications, written with a light touch, such as those by Miss Manners. Your child will bless your foresight when he first dines at a young lady's home, or lunches with his boss.

Involve every member of the family in decisions about the menu and preparation of the meal.

Occasionally have a "Friends of the Family" evening, when anyone in the family can invite a friend.

Food as a Focal Point

Keep junk food to a minimum. Carefully select fresh, healthful natural foods.

QUICK BREAKFAST IDEAS: fresh fruit, scrambled or soft boiled eggs, whole grain toast with butter, oatmeal, grain cereal, granola, or millet, whole grain toast with peanut butter.

QUICK LUNCH IDEAS: peanut butter and jam sandwich, tuna sandwich, egg sandwich, hot dog sandwich, hamburger sandwich, meatloaf sandwich. Soup, chili, or stew in a thermos, chicken legs, chicken salad sandwich, green salad, turkey with corn chips, refried beans with corn tortilla chips, dinner leftovers.

SNACK IDEAS: rice cakes with peanut butter, vegetables with dip, tortilla chips with beans, soup, watermelon or cantaloupe, applesauce, chicken leg, raw nuts or seeds, trail mix, banana with peanut butter, yogurt, carrot sticks, bell pepper slices, jicama, black olives, tortilla chips, small box of raisins, dried fruit (small amounts), fresh fruit, celery with peanut butter, cauliflower, broccoli, popcorn with melted butter and honey.

EASY WAYS TO ENTERTAIN AND TEACH
YOUR CHILDREN AT THE SAME TIME

Motivational Activities

Make your child's dreams and aspirations real. Help her construct a Treasure Map of Her Life Goals. You need a large poster board, glue, and imagination — hers and yours.

First discuss what she would like to have, be, or do this year, next year, the following year, and on into the future. Then let her draw a map of the years, with a separate block for each individual year. Help her find tiny objects or magazine pictures representing her desires so she can glue them on the appropriate years. Resist the inclination to explain why her dreams are impractical. They're her dreams. So next year she wants to be an astronaut. What do you know about it? You're just the technical advisor.

When the Treasure Map is completed, hang it in her room. Let it serve her as a visual inspiration to work toward her goals.

Instructional Activities

Talk to your child about your work, its purpose, how you do it, who you work with, what tools or equipment you use and, if restricted or hazardous working conditions rule out taking her to work with you, stop by with her on your day off. If possible, bring some work home and, if it's something she can help with, do it together.

When a child knows what you do, she can form a mental picture of you at work, and she feels emotionally closer even when you are not with her.

Initiate projects with a chemistry set, ant farm, or model airplane kit.

Watch television with her. Research indicates that television affects children more positively when they watch with adults with whom they can talk about the program. Interaction with adults helps the child distinguish between the reality of the home situation and the illusion of the screen.

Let me suggest, too, that you check the National Public Television stations. They carry high-quality instructional, scientific, and nature programs of interest to children.

Attend a play together, and follow it with a discussion. Taryn and I recently saw a non-traditional interpretation of *You're a Good Man Charlie Brown* in which the childish cartoon characters, including Snoopy, were portrayed by adults in conservative attire. We both enjoyed the play. But at first, Taryn resisted the fact that Snoopy did not look like a dog.

This gave me an opportunity to talk with her about the meaning of the play and, as a graduate of the Age of Aquarius, I found myself in the unusual position of defending the distortion of one of its most venerable symbols. I explained that a director changes a play because he wants to tell us something, and she understood the idea. We agreed that Paul Blake, who directed this particular production, may have wanted to tell us that even though adults look different from cartoon characters, they can have the same thoughts and feelings.

Taryn and I never got around to reading the play itself, but you might consider getting a group together and reading a play aloud, each person reading a part. The readers don't all have to be children. Call in family members or neighbors. If you have more parts than readers, follow the example of short-handed repertory companies. Double up on the parts. If there's only two of you, each can read several parts.

You might also want to consider reading a book together, each reading a separate paragraph, or page, or chapter.

Establish a Family Art Gallery (any wall or section thereof) for the public exhibition of works of art produced by members of the family. Do not let the gallery degenerate into a public bulletin board lest it lose it's distinctive "art gallery" character; hang nothing but art. (I recommend a broad interpretation of the word "art." My definition is: "If the artist says it's art, it's art.") The gallery should admit individual works or collaborations, works in any medium produced at home or at school, collages made from newspapers, magazines, tin cans, or souvenirs from outings.

If you find sufficient community (family) interest, you could make an exception to the family-only stipulation and set aside a Visiting Artist Section to hang newspaper and magazine copies of great works. It could provide a painless and humanized introduction to art.

Family Unity

Plan together, as a family: vacation trips, birthday parties, and holiday celebrations, Christmas, Hanukkah, New Year's. Take the whole family trick-or-treating on Halloween.

Plan an old-fashioned evening at home. No television, no radio, no records and, if you want to give it real character, no electric lights during dinner, just candles. A simple meal, cooked at home with family cooperation, followed by reading, games, and group singing; the kind of warm gathering that, in retrospect, frequently becomes a treasured symbol of family affection and solidarity.

Get dressed up and go to a nice restaurant together.

Call the local chamber of commerce and ask them to send a brochure describing points of interest in the area. You'll be surprised how many interesting places you've forgotten about or never been to. Take short trips or one-day outings.

Start a Family Scrapbook Project. You've seen the books in every stationery store. I recommend a really big scrapbook, one that can handle the memorabilia from all the parties, vacations, birthdays, picnics, graduations, and school events.

Also initiate a Family Photograph Album Project. You can pick up an album at any department or stationery store. As each photograph is entered, add a note identifying the people, the occasion, and the date. I advise against informal identification. "Butch at the picnic" is clear to us right now, but it won't mean much as the years pass. Children and grandchildren will bless you for your thoughtfulness in providing solid data like "Jim 'Butch' Gallagher at Oakland Elks Picnic. 6/7/1990."

Pick up an inexpensive video machine and record your experiences together. Take a tape recorder along on trips to record comments and you will see how much fun you'll have listening to the playback.

Sports and Hobbies, Outdoors or Indoors

Go ice skating, roller skating, bowling, fishing, or swimming together. Or attend professional sports events.

If you play on a baseball, softball, or volleyball team, bring the children to your games.

If you collect coins, stamps, butterflies, or antiques, or if you are interested in magic, let them work with you.

Go for walks together. It's a great way to get out in the air, exercise, and enjoy nature. And it's a great time to talk.

Join them in their interests: scouting, Little League, or tennis.

ACTIVITIES CHILDREN CAN
ENJOY WITH OTHERS

Broad exposure to people and activities outside the family circle teaches the socialization and teamwork crucial to survival in a civilized society. It is essential to the full development of every child, particularly an only child.

Divorced fathers, without realizing it, are prone to monopolize a child's time, depriving her of normal developmental experiences and stifling her social development.

Check with your local recreation centers, YWCA, YMCA, Little League, tennis clubs, schools, athletic associations, dancing studios, and libraries, and take a look at their group activities. You'll find a group activity menu to whet any child's appetite.

DANCE: ballet, tap, aerobics, square, ballroom.
MUSIC: choir, orchestra, band, musical comedies.
MARTIAL ARTS: karate, aikido, judo.
SPORTS: Pop Warner football, Little League, swimming, baseball, softball, volleyball, wrestling, soccer, tennis.

ACTIVITIES CHILDREN CAN ENJOY BY THEMSELVES

Encourage Individual Play

Much as a child seeks our attention, and much as we love being with her, other matters incessantly demand our time. It's probably life's way of giving a child time to be alone and develop the inner resources she will need throughout her life. Encourage independent play. It leads to self-reliance, independence, and creativity.

Keep an age-appropriate selection of the following items on hand and easily accessible to your children.

Crayons, pencils, felt markers, chalk and board, pens, colored construction paper, watercolors and finger paints, brushes, paper tablets.

Stapler, hole punch, scissors, measuring spoons, paper clips, paste, tape, rubber bands, string, pipe cleaners, toothpicks, straws, popsicle sticks, aluminum foil.

Ribbons, glitter, buttons, shells, corks, cotton balls, marbles, carpet squares, styrofoam pieces, cardboard tubes, sponges, bottle caps.

Coffee cans, empty plastic bottles, milk cartons, jars, paper cups, aluminum pie pans, paper towels, extra sheet (for fort or tent).

Check All Toys for Safety

Examine all toys before you let your child play with them, the toys that are given to her as well as the ones you buy for her. Pay attention to unsafe toy warnings issued by consumers' reports, radio and television stations, newspapers, magazines, mothers' clubs, and health departments.

Keep all unsafe toys including the following out of her hands:
▷ Toys with sharp points or edges.
▷ Glass toys of any kind.
▷ Toys that are smaller than your fist.
▷ Stuffed animals whose eyes can be pulled out, or that have other easily removable parts.

Age Appropriate Toys

Most better (and by better I mean conscientious) toy manufacturers indicate the age ranges of their products. The following overall guide should be helpful in selecting toys not so identified. Your child's interests and skill levels can dictate modification of this generally applicable list.

INFANCY (Birth to eighteen months) — Stuffed animals, crib-exercisers, stacking toys, nursery mobiles, floating bath toys, large balls, large blocks, books with pictures and music, toys for pounding, teething rings, rattles, musical toys.

EIGHTEEN MONTHS TO THREE YEARS — Sand box, large crayons, play furniture, large-piece puzzles, carpentry tools, play calculator, hobby horse, pails and shovels, stuffed animals, swings and climbing equipment, tape recorder, kitchen utensil toys, simple musical instruments, pull toys, dolls and doll furniture.

THREE TO SIX YEARS — Card games, books, play sets, toy records and record player, puzzles, sewing machine, wagon, puppets, blocks, small trucks, airplanes, cars, boats, slide projector.

SIX TO NINE YEARS — Skates, erector and construction sets, advanced books, dolls and doll houses, racing sets, print set, table games, advanced carpentry sets, board games, typewriter.

NINE TO TWELVE YEARS — Computer games, model sets, chemistry sets, card games, auto race sets.

Chapter 10

Discipline

*As individuals we know that the law which
restrains us likewise protects us.*

— Dag Hammarskjold

ESTABLISHING LOVE AND ORDER

Discipline is not Punishment

A good word, like a good person, can pick up a bad reputation by associating with wicked words. Unfortunately the thoroughly respectable word "discipline" has been hanging out with punishment for so long that people take them for twins. They're not.

When you punish, you impose a penalty (discomfort, loss, suffering) on a wrongdoer. When you discipline a young person, on the other hand, you help him develop orderliness, efficiency, self-control, and character, starting him on a path that can lead to his becoming a member of his community to the mutual benefit of himself and the community.

There are times when judicious punishment is essential to the child's safety, but the occasions are rare, and on the whole, we're talking about discipline, not punishment.

As parents we are inclined to be impatient about discipline because we take a short view of it. We think of it only as a solution to today's problem: "I don't know what I'm going to do with that kid of mine. No matter how many times I told him, he still doesn't put his toys away." So you finally give up and do it yourself, and that's where discipline ends, right where it should have begun.

You took care of the problem for the moment, and at the same time you taught your child to be irresponsible. Twenty years down the road you'll wonder why he dropped out of school, never finishes anything he starts, can't hold a job, and is always in debt and in trouble. You missed the main point of discipline, and he will miss the main point of Ghandi's words: "The highest form of freedom carries with it the greatest measure of discipline. . . . Unbridled license is. . . injurious alike to self and one's neighbors."

You May Revolt Against Discipline

Under the most idyllic family conditions, discipline is difficult. Divorce makes it worse. You may back off because your self-esteem is so ravaged that you clutch desperately at your child's love, fearing anything that may turn him against you. Or you may feel that your failure to hold the marriage together is responsible for the child's plight, and think you should repay him by making his life more pleasant. Or his short visits may become so precious that you don't want to darken a single minute with discipline.

Your Child May Revolt Against Lack of Discipline

Your child doesn't understand your emotions or your motives. All he knows is that everything is going wrong and he feels awful. Night and day the recurrent shadowy terror of abandonment, of being lost in an alien and threatening wilderness, plagues him. But he lacks the skill to formulate the idea clearly, let alone communicate it to you. He doesn't know how to stage a strike, or mount a consumer protest, or organize a public demonstration.

So he screams, primitive and incoherent, demanding an end to uncertainty and ambiguity, a restoration of love and order, and his screams may take many forms: he may demonstrate any of the physical or mental danger signals discussed elsewhere in this book. His behavior may become negative, obstinate, and erratic, or anxious, servile, overly affectionate, and dependent. He may become hyperactive or withdrawn. He may follow you around and not let you out of his sight, or he may avoid you.

To a child, lack of discipline is like a race with no starting point, no ending point, and no judges. Children always need a discernible, consistent pattern of discipline with clear rules and regulations that direct and limit their behavior. The need intensifies after a divorce, because discipline extends continuity and predictability into a world otherwise out of control. They need to know that parents, even though they are divorced from each other, are not divorced from the children. They need to know that both parents still care enough to set and enforce limits.

DISCIPLINE IN ACTION

Discipline is part of your total relationship with, and responsibility to, your child. As a parent, you are, by nature and law, his protector. While he is under your care, you are the final authority on his discipline. You can delegate the carrying out of specific areas of your responsibility to teachers and babysitters, and share some areas with your wife, but you cannot relinquish it in full to anyone.

Discipline must be closely coordinated with everyone involved. Keep your child's mother advised of all discipline problems encountered and corrective action taken while the child is with you. It will save you from working at cross purposes, assure the child more coherent discipline, and discourage him from using the two of you against each other to see where he can get the better deal. Work closely with your wife to coordinate discipline within your own home.

Discipline must be consistent. Rewards must be appropriate to the behavior they reward, and punishments must be appropriate to the behavior they punish. Don't weaken your credibility by offering a reward or threatening a punishment and not carrying through.

Don't overdo talk. Children understand action better. If your child is consistently late for dinner, call him twice, then take his plate away. No dinner tonight. He won't starve.

Be a good role model to your child. As the adage goes, your actions speak louder than your words. He will do as you do, not as you say. Act as you want him to act.

When you say "No" to him, say it with conviction and without personal discomfort. If you are uncomfortable in your mind, he will hear it in your voice, and your authority will crumble. You can't fool him. It's like walking up to an uncaged tiger and saying, "You d-d-don't s-s-scare me."

Expect your child to challenge your rules to see if you really mean them, to see how far he can go. Such testing is essential to his growth. Soon he will have to test the world, and he can't learn overnight. He should start young and practice on you, just as lion cubs practice on their parents. Your best defense against his challenge is carefully thought out discipline, with appropriate consequences consistently applied.

Forfeit the cherished American illusion that you can be buddy and father. You can't play both roles at the same time. If you elect the role of buddy, you become his equal, and you will fail him when he needs discipline. He will not accept discipline from an equal. I offer what I hope is a consoling thought: your child will have lots of buddies but only one father.

Keep your discipline free of anger and base it on love. Make it clear that your love for him is eternal; you love him and always will. You may hate something he does, but you will never hate him.

And your rules and the consequences of violating them must be age-related, and capable of being easily understood and followed by anyone your child's age.

B. F. SKINNER'S OPERANT CONDITIONING

B. F. Skinner, one of America's most respected and controversial behavioral psychologists, made a clean break with the established everything's-in-your-mind psychoanalytic school. His theories were revolutionary when he introduced them in 1938. Now they are standard practice in fields as divergent as education, smoking and diet control, the treatment of schizophrenic patients, and the rehabilitation of delinquent adolescents.

Please give some thought to Skinner's Theory of Operant Conditioning. It's clearcut and pragmatic and, to Skinner's credit, it makes common sense respectable.

We'll look at Skinner's theory shortly. But first, a few of his central concepts; they will make the theory easier to understand.

A *Reinforcement* is any reward that increases the probability that a desired behavior will be repeated. In our society, the word reward evokes visions of cash money. Skinner's use of the term includes an infinitely broader range of possibilities.

A *Positive Reinforcement* is a material (cookie, coin, gold star, trinket, book) or non-material (attention, smile, a pat on the shoulder) reward.

A *Negative Reinforcement* is the withdrawal of something that creates discomfort or pain.

A *Punishment* is the application of something that creates discomfort. It is the opposite of a negative reinforcement because it applies rather than withdraws discomfort. This is a subtle distinction, but an important one.

Now for the theory, as it applies to our interest in discipline.

Theory: When a child exhibits approved behavior, reinforcement (positive or negative) will increase the likelihood that he will repeat the approved behavior.

Example: Reinforcing desired behavior. When your older child plays gently with your younger child, and you reward his behavior with a positive or negative reinforcer, the older child is more apt to continue this behavior.

Example: Reinforcing undesired behavior. Skinner finds that reinforcement can also, unintentionally, encourage behavior you don't want. If a child throws a tantrum, for instance, to get his father's attention, the child is more likely to repeat the tantrum if the father pays attention to him (rewards him with attention) and less likely if the father ignores him.

Theory: Mild punishment when combined with a demonstration of an alternate approved behavior, will increase the likelihood that he will duplicate the approved behavior.

Example: When your older child is rough with your younger child, and you punish him (slap his hand) and then demonstrate how to play gently, the older child may exchange the roughness for gentle play, encouraged by two reinforcers, first your approval and, second, the pleasure of playing with the child.

Theory: Mild punishment alone may suppress undesired behavior, but frequently a child will resort to trickery or deceit rather than decrease the undesired behavior.

Example: When your older child is rough with your younger child, and you punish him (slap his wrist), he may discontinue the behavior in your presence but pinch the younger child behind your back.

Theory: Strong punishment repeated whenever an undesirable behavior is demonstrated can completely suppress the behavior. It may, however, severely affect the child. He may develop an avoidance response that will become generalized to the entire situation.

Example: A youngster who is severely punished for playing roughly with a younger child may avoid the child the rest of his life because of the pain he associates with the child.

Theory: If a child is placed in an unresolvable conflict between the pleasure of undesirable behavior and the fear of the harsh punishment associated with the behavior, he may become neurotic.

Example: This syndrome not uncommonly results from severe punishment for undesirable sexual behavior.

Skinner's research also indicates that the more immediate a response, the stronger its effect. The more time that intervenes between your child's behavior and your response, the less effect your response will have.

Skinner's work on the value of immediate response is, in my opinion, one of his finest contributions to modern psychology. I suggest that you, as a father, give immediate attention to immediate response. When your child's behavior calls for reinforcement or punishment, act as quickly as you can. The sooner you respond, the more easily he will connect his action and your response, and the more likely you are to get results.

UNACCEPTABLE PUNISHMENT

Two forms of punishment are never justifiable. Mental abuse is one of them. Never shame, ridicule, or humiliate your child under any circumstances, whether you are alone with him or in front of friends, teachers, or family members. A child's lack of sophistication and need for approval lays his self-image open to permanent distortion by an acid tongue. Save the backhanded bitterness for adults who can handle it.

The other unacceptable punishment is physical abuse. Any time you spank harder than you intended, any time you find yourself becoming more angry as you spank, any time you have difficulty stopping, you are in danger of inflicting physical damage. Stop immediately, and do not touch your child again unless you are positive you are in full control of your feelings.

You can inflict physical abuse without leaving a mark or a scar, but if you ever strike your child in the face, or create welts, bruises, or abrasions, you are absolutely out of control. Call a crisis line immediately and get help. This is not a situation you can handle alone. Knowledgeable, understanding people, who have been through it themselves, wait at the other end of the telephone line, ready to help. Call them.

PHYSICAL DISCIPLINE

Some authorities feel that physical discipline can psychologically harm a child and should never be used. Others recommend its limited use from ages say two to ten, at which time the child's reasoning and verbal skills should be sufficiently mature to eliminate the need for physical discipline; the need decreasing as the age increases. From my experience with children, I agree with the latter opinion.

My agreement, however, is restricted to two forms of physical discipline. The first is spanking, and by this I mean a slap to a well-padded bottom. This action is acceptable only when you must restrain or protect your child from imminent danger, and when it is the only way to make your point quickly, clearly, and directly.

The other is a tap of the finger on the arm, hand, or fingers. Never slap or tap your child with any object, such as a ruler. Eliminating the human contact strips the act of humanity. This action is warranted only when patient reasoning fails, and when the child persists in mischief, disobedience, aggression, or willful destruction of property.

Physical discipline should not be used unless all other means have been exhausted. It should never be used in anger, and you should always explain your reason to the child.

Chapter 11

Your Child's Chores and Allowance

*Just as an allowance is a child's share of the family
income, a chore is his share of the family life.*
— Jean Ross Peterson, *It Doesn't Grow on Trees* [1]

YOUR CHILD'S CHORES

Social Contract

In a democracy like the United States, individuals live under a
"Social Contract" form of government in which they voluntarily sur-
render part of their "natural" freedom to the government (e.g., pay
taxes) in return for the benefits of living in an organized state (e.g.,
police protection). The family operates under an implicit social contract. Ideally, each member voluntarily contributes. Chores should be
treated as a child's contribution in return for the benefits of living in
a family, and these chores should be done in a spirit of voluntary cooperation.

Children Should Not Be Paid For Chores

To confirm each member's obligation to contribute to, and right
to benefit from, the family, and to maintain a spirit of voluntary cooperation, regular chores should be performed without payment.

Make a clear distinction between allowance and chores. It is important that the child understand: 1) The allowance is hers. It is a
benefit she receives from the family, and it does not depend on completion of chores. 2) The chores are an obligation she owes the family
group. Payment can, of course, be made for special tasks which are
not classified as a part of the child's chores.

When to Start Assigning Chores

The sooner children begin helping with chores, the sooner they
feel like an integral part of the family, and many child authorities

consider two an ideal age to start. At two, children are eager, if seldom adept. They can dust large surfaces and, as they get a little older, they can help set and clear the table, and make their own beds.

Explain Chores

Chores are the first phase of an individual's lifetime working career. You're not teaching your child to dust a coffee table. You're teaching her to believe in her own ability to learn, to understand and follow instructions, to find satisfaction and pleasure in work. You're not training her for today; you're training her for tomorrow.

Talk on the child's eye level. If you want her to dust the coffee table, kneel on the floor by the table as you talk so she can look into your face. Break the job into small, separate steps, then show-and-tell: demonstrate a step as you explain it. Let the child do it herself before you go on to the next step. Seeing and understanding are the first stages of learning. Real learning is in the doing.

Resist the impulse to finish the job yourself. It will damage her self-confidence, and decrease her ability to learn.

Always encourage. Overlook failures. Search out successes, no matter how small or marginal. Find something to praise and praise it.

Encourage a positive attitude toward work by taking a positive attitude yourself. Your child will learn to enjoy what you enjoy.

Appropriate Children's Chores

Chores are regularly assigned tasks that represent the child's share of the work done by the family, so the family's work will determine the nature of the child's chores. For that reason, the following "starting" and "advanced" chores are offered as general, rather than specific, suggestions.

STARTING CHORES

Kitchen: Stack, wash, and dry dishes, put dishes away, polish silver, sweep and wash floors, clean counters and table tops, empty trash, clean out refrigerator.

Living Room and Bedrooms: Straighten up, dust, empty trash, water plants, polish furniture.

Bathroom: Pick up, clean mirrors, counters, tubs, showers, sinks, scrub toilets, wash floors, empty trash.

Outside: Sweep steps, pick up papers, weed garden.

ADVANCED CHORES

Inside: Cook, shop, sew, babysit younger children and help with homework, assist in entertaining, interior decoration, minor electrical, painting, carpentry, and plumbing jobs, do laundry, vacuum, wash windows.

Outside: Mow lawn, trim hedges, wax car and perform minor repairs and maintenance.

Assigning Chores

Be flexible. Adjust the schedule so it works for everyone.

If the children agree to cooperate, permit each child to select and commit to the chores she will do. Let them know that lack of cooperation will result in assignment of chores by lot or by your arbitrary decision. Change chore responsibilities often.

Whenever possible, schedule chores immediately before an activity the children like. It gives them something to look forward to, motivates them to get the work done, and forms a pleasant association between work and play.

Publishing Chores

Post a Chore Schedule containing a complete list for each family member in a central location, such as the kitchen or family room. Each chore must be clearly stated, and be accompanied by all pertinent information (day, time, deadline) needed to establish mutual understanding within the family, and avoid misinterpretation, e.g., vacuum dining room and living room carpets every Monday and Friday before five p.m. Failure to prepare this list carefully and correctly will lead to disputes about responsibility and create endless family bickering.

Responding to Complaints

Before you respond, evaluate the complaint. A complaint is justified if: 1) a child is assigned tasks beyond her mental or physical ability; 2) she is required to do more than her share of work. Some children fall victim to the will-you-give-me-a-hand syndrome because they're always there at the moment. Others become victims of the work-a-good-horse-to-death philosophy because they are more competent.

When the complaint is justified you owe the child an apology and an adjustment, the sooner the better.

Punishing Nonperformance

If the child refuses to do his chores, appropriate punishment, as previously established, must be administered. Punishment (and by this I never mean physical or mental punishment) must be as specific and clear as the chores themselves. Everyone must know what the consequences will be if he or she fails to perform assigned chores.

YOUR CHILD'S ALLOWANCE

Your child's allowance is her first experience in money management, her first step toward financial independence. It is your statement of respect for her growing ability to handle her own affairs. Your child's allowance is, most of all, a no-strings expression of your unqualified love for her.

"Money should never be used to manipulate a child's behavior," according to Jean Ross Peterson, an authority on the subject. If an allowance is an unconditional right of the child by reason of his membership in the family, to share in the family income, then it can no more be made contingent upon the child's behavior or actions than the family membership itself.

The Question of Duplicate Allowances

When your child doesn't live with you all the time, the question arises whether one or both parents should take care of the allowance.

In this, as in any matter affecting the child, divorced parents should coordinate their actions to discourage the child from playing them against each other. The parents should jointly agree on the total amount of allowance, and each should separately provide half that amount to the child. To a child, an allowance is a tangible statement of fidelity and love, and any child, but especially a child of divorce, cannot be reassured too frequently.

When to Start an Allowance

A child should begin to receive an allowance as soon as she learns to count, and she should receive it every week on the same day of the week.

Appropriate Amount of Allowance

The child's allowance is part of the family budget, and the amount should be determined when overall budget decisions are made. It should be sufficient to cover small nonessential items, snacks, and inexpensive toys. As the child grows, the allowance, too, should grow. A teen's allowance should cover recreation, lunches, dates, and clothes. I agree with Jean Ross Peterson's statement: "If the purpose of an allowance is to give children the skills and values for sound money management and effective consumerism, then a child should use his income for both luxuries and necessities."

Chapter 12

Stamping Out Manipulation

Our chief want in life is somebody who will
make us do what we can.

— Ralph Waldo Emerson

I remember the dreadful times when Taryn would start crying as soon as she saw me. She would pull back, hide behind her mother, and scream that she did not want to come with me. She resisted getting into my car with all the furious force of her small body. Then she would insist that her mother come and virtually tuck her into the car.

When your child acts as though you are kidnapping her, your heart breaks. To make it worse, my former wife would bend over and whisper, "When you come home, I'll have a nice surprise waiting for you." In effect bribing my own child to spend time with me. Dogged determination alone contained my tears.

Then one day, not fifteen seconds after we pulled away from the curb, Taryn reverted to the loving little girl I knew. She was, in fact, more affectionate than usual, and I worried about the possibility that guilt motivated her lavish attention.

My worry and her guilt soon dissipated as we crunched along the sun-dazzled sand, her brightly clad little body skittering like a butterfly at the ocean's rim, her satiny little hand confidently holding mine. Her eyes would widen in wonder at the massive blue-green waves and the dancing- diamond sparkles of the surf, and her serious little face occasionally turned to me in comment or question.

Later, as I sat alone in my apartment, the worry returned un-summoned, but with it came an answer: Taryn's mother, like many divorced mothers, was undoubtedly unhappy about handing the child over to her father. This unhappiness had transmitted itself to Taryn, who in turn sensed that if she accepted responsibility for leaving, she would have to accept the guilt of creating her mother's unhappiness. The weight of that guilt drove her to reject responsibility by demonstrating that she was leaving under protest.

Taryn had, consciously or unconsciously, contrived these dramatic parting scenes as a peace offering to her mother, proof that her departure was involuntary. And my concealed but intuitively perceived pain had complicated and fueled the self-perpetuating emotional cycle.

Both Taryn and I had been manipulated: Taryn by her mother's unhappiness, me by Taryn's resultant rejection. My new insight decreased my pain and allowed me to concentrate on Taryn's problem. In place of frozen distress signals, I now responded to her tantrums with acceptance and cheerful anticipation of a great day. The scenes continued for a while and they still hurt, but gradually they lessened and then just faded away.

Recently, I picked Taryn up under very different circumstances. She sat primly upright on the edge of a large chair, ladylike and proper as only a self-confident five year old can be. She chatted contentedly for a few minutes with me and my former spouse — obviously a child who felt no clash between herself and her mother, nor between her mother and father. Then she turned to me, and said, "Shall we go now?"

Silently I gave thanks for the insight that had come to me uninvited and unexpected. Without it I might well have become discouraged, accepted Taryn's rejection at face value, and given up. And today could never have happened.

MANIPULATION'S MANY DISGUISES

I do not want to imply that Taryn's mother consciously said to herself: "I think I'll perform a little manipulation here, to make sure things come out my way." She was probably trying to cope, the best way she knew, with the storms that rage around child custody. I do want to point out the invidious nature of the manipulation to which these storms give birth.

Manipulation, like a virus, can enter and take control of a person without that person's knowledge or consent, or like a spider web, it can be the well-crafted child of instinct. Or, it can, like a grand masterpiece, be intentionally planned, designed, and executed to achieve a precise effect. Like the Greek god Zeus, who transformed himself at will into anything from a gentle swan to a raging bull, manipulation comes in many disguises. Among the very young, it is most frequently seen as:

Manipulation by Tantrum, e.g., "I'm holding my breath until you buy me that doll." (I'll win because you can't bear to stand there and let me die).

Manipulation by Flattery, e.g., "You're the most wonderful, funny, happy, handsome, loveable daddy in the whole wide world." (I wanna go to the movies.)

Manipulation by Malingering, e.g., "I hurt all over. I'm too sick to go to school." (I didn't do my homework.)

Manipulation by Comparison, e.g., "Mommy isn't mean. She lets me eat ice cream for breakfast every day." (You better, too, or you'll lose the popularity contest.)

Manipulation by Deception, e.g., "I didn't lose my watch. Somebody stole it." (I'm off the hook.)

SHIELD YOURSELF FROM MANIPULATION BY YOUR CHILD

Don't mistake unintentional manipulation for the real thing. A child can babble on about what a wonderful time she always has with mommy or about the nice men in mommy's life. Such pain, if maliciously inflicted by an adult, would warrant a challenge to swords at dawn. But your child can innocently stab you through the heart, blind to the blade handle protruding from your chest, unaware of the blood seeping through your shirt, as guiltless of intent as the rug you just tripped over.

Let me give you an example. Taryn and I had spent a wonderful day in the open, in tune with nature and with each other. We sauntered beneath the arching pink and white cherry blossoms of the Japanese Garden; leaned on the rustic redwood bridge rail watching scores of carp gliding in the water below, red-gold, white, and lemon-yellow, sunbursts of enameled glitter. We picnicked in the park, followed by ice cream at the stand.

Followed by bedtime, when Taryn began crying for her mother.

Followed by an ugly suspicion, emanating from the pit of my stomach, that I had stepped on something very much like a land mine. My developing companionship with my child, my growing competence as a father, my plans, my dreams — exploded, shattered, strewn about the landscape. In spite of all my efforts, in spite of my belief that I was getting to be a pretty good father, I must be only a second-rate father. My child did not love me as much as she loved her mother.

Afterward, calmly rethinking the disaster, I felt a resurgence of confidence. It was not, after all, a competition. It was natural for a child who had spent most of her time at home with her mother to cry for the familiar security, especially after a long and tiring day. There, I felt better. Not good, but better.

The same actions, by a different child, or the same child under different circumstances and with a different motivation could clearly be manipulation; this was not. It was the child's direct response to insecurity.

RESPOND TO UNINTENTIONAL AND INTENTIONAL MANIPULATION THE SAME WAY

Dealing with manipulation is one of the very few times I suggest that you not openly discuss your feelings with your child. In many instances it is helpful to you and to her to discuss how you feel about what she has done or said; this is not one of them.

If you tell her how bad she made you feel, even if it was unintentional, you will be telling her that she accidentally stumbled on a way to control you. Don't hand her a control and not expect her to use it. It's like handing her money and not expecting her to spend it. If it was intentional, and you admit how bad you feel, you will reinforce the tendency to manipulate.

Either way, you injure your child. Manipulation, being essentially devious, in addition to corrupting her relationship with you, can create guilt about her dishonesty. And in the long term, the child in whom manipulation is encouraged, frequently becomes a manipulative adult, tainting all of her adult relationships.

Never respond as you would to an adult, never show emotion or pain, never ask for further information. Never encourage the conversation, never show any interest whatsoever, never indicate by word or expression that you think manipulation is cute or clever (even if it is). Never let the child overhear you relating the incident to other adults (especially in an amused or approving tone of voice).

Always remove yourself emotionally from the situation, respond in the detached tone you would use to a chance stranger who had been kind enough to give you the correct time. Always acknowledge what she has said. Let her know that you heard her and you understand. That's it. And move on quickly to another subject. Distract her attention. Many a time have I thanked nature for the short attention span she so graciously bestowed on the very young.

SHIELD YOUR CHILD FROM MANIPULATION BY HER MOTHER

The problem of protecting your child against manipulation by her mother does not stand alone. It is an essential segment of your pattern of transactions with your former wife and it requires the same rational and ethical approach we discussed in the section on child-centered parenting partnerships. If you are currently faced by a manipulation problem, flip back to Chapter 3 and scan the parenting partnership material.

You will find that a manipulation problem differs from your everyday run-of-the-mill issue in two ways. First, it is more difficult to pin down. You can know what's going on without being able to prove it. Here's where you use your detective skills. When you feel that the child is being manipulated, stop. Ask yourself, what evidence do I have? And then your common sense — is the child acting, talking, feeling uncharacteristically? Does she appear to be reacting to information to which she did not personally have access? Was that information known to her mother? Is she claiming, without factual basis, an attitude which in reality belongs to her mother?

The second difference is an offshoot of the first. Frequently, the child has supplied your only available evidence. Here you have a decision to make. If you face the mother with your child's statement and she, as a result, scolds the child for tattling, you assume certain risks. The child, sensing her power position, may use the two of you against each other for her own objectives. Or she may turn secretive and keep everything from you. Or she may experience fear or guilt. Any way you turn, the result could be destructive to your child's character, her emotional health, or your relationship with her.

If, on the other hand, you play it safe and say nothing, the manipulation will continue.

I found myself in exactly this position when I picked Taryn up late one Christmas Eve. She was to spend the next two days with me and I wanted these days, especially Santa's arrival, to be enchanted — just as magic for her as it was, years ago, for me.

When she was securely strapped into the car seat, and we were on our way, I began creating a holiday ambience. "Santa," I was explaining, "will come down the chimney in his red and white suit, with loads and loads of presents for . . ." A little voice at my side had interrupted me. "Mommy says that Santa Claus doesn't come to daddy's house." While I was explaining Santa's change of plans (I had checked with him an hour ago, and he said he would be there at midnight), I was thinking, how ridiculous! A couple of nine year olds would be humiliated to be caught in this conversation.

"Santa doesn't come to your house."

"He does too!"

"Does not. He only comes to my house."

"That's what you think. He told me he changed his plans."

I decided that a confrontation to put an end to this foolishness was potentially less damaging to Taryn than continued manipulation. Having decided to call Taryn's mother, and following my own advice, I made notes of exactly what I wanted to say, including a brief description of the manipulative activity and its potential injury to the child.

As soon as Taryn was busy out of earshot, I placed the call. I held it to the one subject, and kept it courteous, unemotional, and short. I stated that I refused to be an active or passive participant, and demanded that the manipulation be stopped.

That was my decision in that particular instance, and it seems to have turned out well. That is not to indicate that you would, or should, have acted similarly. Each father must decide each case, based on his knowledge of the people involved and the particular circumstances.

Regardless of how you handle manipulation problems with your former wife, your most urgent responsibility remains to try to keep your child clear of emotional entanglement in it.

SHIELD YOUR CHILD FROM YOUR MANIPULATION

"From me?" you exclaim. "Me who wants nothing more than my child's happiness? Me who has spent years fighting for the right to protect and guide her? Not me, surely!"

Yes, you and me. We love our children, and our love makes us vulnerable. We know fathers who have been unjustly separated from their children, and we are sufficiently realistic to know it could happen to us. We have seen our father-child relationships threatened by the courts or other less formal, if more virulent, influences, and we have known overwhelming powerlessness.

Herein lies the danger. Brute strength, whether physical or legal, can enforce its will directly. The powerless are driven to achieve their ends by stealth and manipulation, by nature duplicitous.

Should desperation tempt you to use this tool; should the thought cross your mind that a word here or a hint there could redress the wrongs done you or your child; should it seem the only answer — back away. Better to lose a point than to set her an example of manipulation.

Chapter 13

Finding the Right Babysitter

Little children are still the symbol of the eternal marriage between love and duty.

— George Eliot

Until your child is sufficiently independent, mature, responsible, and resourceful to care for and protect herself, you need a babysitter to supervise her in your absence. Everyday observation of her awareness of, and ability to respond intelligently to, danger will tell you when she has graduated from the babysitting stage.

Conditions other than your daughter's ability may determine the need for a babysitter. If you are in a high crime area, or if there are known rapists or child molesters about, you may need to retain the babysitter longer. If, on the other hand, your apartment or house is surrounded on all sides by watchful, concerned, and caring neighbors, you may be able to dispense with babysitting services earlier.

You need a babysitter who is responsible and trustworthy, and has sufficient good sense and experience to know what to do in an emergency. She must be actively with your child, not on the telephone with her boyfriend while your child investigates the kitchen cabinet. She must understand the difference between a babysitter and a housesitter, and should think of herself as a responsible child supervisor, rather than a passive visitor.

HOW TO FIND A BABYSITTER

Friends and neighbors are an excellent source because they have firsthand knowledge of you, your children, and what kind of person you want to supervise your child.

Your neighborhood church may be aware of appropriate individuals in the area.

Contact neighborhood youth organizations, recreation departments, the YMCA.

Check with preschools. Members of their staff frequently babysit privately.

Most hotels and motels maintain a register of qualified sitters as a service for their guests. They may give you names and telephone numbers.

College student-employment offices usually have a substantial list of students who supplement their income by babysitting.

Screen Background Thoroughly

QUESTIONS TO ASK THE PROSPECTIVE SITTER:

▷ Does she like children? Enjoy babysitting? Would she prefer another kind of work?

▷ How much babysitting experience has she had?

▷ What kind of problems or emergencies has she encountered? How did she handle them?

▷ What kind of emergencies has she run into, and how did she handle them?

▷ Has she taken first aid or child development courses?

▷ What would she do if there were an earthquake, tornado, fire, medical, or poison emergency?

▷ What would she do if there was a knock at the door? If someone called and asked what time you would be back?

▷ Will her parents or other knowledgeable adults be available by telephone in the event she needs help or has a question?

If she seems like the sitter you want, go over the conditions of employment and ask if they are agreeable. If she objects to any condition you deem essential, there's no reason to continue the interview. However, if accommodation would be merely inconvenient, try to find a compromise. A good babysitter is hard to find.

Before you conclude the interview, ask if she has any questions.

Talk with her parents to get a general idea of her background and values. Ask if she babysat for her brothers and sisters or neighborhood children over the years. Do her parents feel she has sufficient experience and resourcefulness to handle the responsibility of a _____ year old child?

Check with former employers and references. Before you ask questions, very briefly state your child's age and explain any unusual condition such as overnight sitting. This is apt to elicit more relevant information; a sitter who would be great for a ten year old might be a disaster with an infant.

Ask former employers to verify dates and duties. Any substantial deviation from the facts should set off a warning alarm in your mind.

Entrusting your child to a person lacking accuracy or veracity would be most unwise.

When the conversation nears conclusion ask, "Would you recommend that I hire (name of applicant) to babysit my (repeat your child's age again) year old child?

Who is Not a Good Babysitter

Your former wife is a last resort only. Never ask her to babysit unless it is a real emergency and it's impossible to find anyone else. In the first place, it doesn't make sense. You spend years in the courts just to get the right to spend time with your child. Then you turn around, hand her the child and say, "Take care of her. I don't have time." Secondly, nothing can rekindle old resentments and angers as quickly as asking her to babysit while you're out on the town.

Your new wife, or if you have not remarried, your very special lady friend is not a babysitter. No matter how much she may care about your child, it is unfair to ask her to care for your child.

BEFORE THE NEW BABYSITTER ARRIVES

Make a last minute safety check. Secure all doors, windows, and screens. Verify that stove, coffeemaker, iron, and similar electrical equipment are off, fireplace logs are out, and air conditioner or heater is properly set.

Prepare written emergency instructions for the babysitter:

▷ Name and telephone number where you can be reached.

▷ Location of first aid kit.

▷ Name and telephone number of alternate responsible adult to call if you cannot be reached.

▷ The time you will return with a notation that, should you be detained by an emergency, the child is not to be left alone. If they cannot reach you, the babysitter is to call the alternate number above or her parents for advice. Should it become necessary to remove the child from the house, she is to leave a note on the floor inside the front door, so you will see it as soon as you come in, saying where the child is and what time they left.

▷ Name, number, and address of person who has a key to your house in case the babysitter and the child accidentally lock themselves out.

▷ Telephone calls should be held to a minimum and be as brief as possible, so the line can be kept open in case of emergencies, or if you need to get in touch with her.

> ▷ Emergency telephone numbers, police, fire, hospital emergency room, poison control office, ambulance.
> ▷ The 911 emergency number with specific instructions to use it only as a last resort.
> ▷ Emergency fire procedures for the babysitter: Remove the child from the house and keep her with you while you call the fire department. Find a safe place for you and the child to stay, in a neighbor's house if possible. Do not return to the house until the police or firemen say you can.

Leave toys and books and games your child enjoys.

If the babysitter intends to do homework when your child is sleeping, prepare a comfortable working area with adequate lighting. It should be in immediate proximity of where your daughter sleeps so the babysitter will hear if she calls or gets up.

Prepare food for your child and the babysitter.

Before Leaving Your Child

Ask the sitter to come fifteen minutes early to allow time to:

Introduce her to your child, the dog, and anyone in the house at the time.

Tour the house with the babysitter and your child. Point out all areas that are off limits, and point out all exits, demonstrating tricky locks or latches. Review fire emergency procedures (above).

Run through the written emergency information with the sitter and, if your child is old enough to understand, have your child join the two of you.

First, go over the rules that apply to your child: bedtime, food, TV time. Next, review those that apply to the babysitter: telephone time, guests. Show the babysitter where the prepared food is.

Ask your child and the sitter if they have any questions they would like you to answer.

The Best Way to Leave is Quickly

You have found a good babysitter. You have made all necessary preparations. You have left thorough instructions.

You have, in short, done everything that can be done. Don't linger. The longer you stay, the more tense your daughter will become about your leaving.

Kiss her. Tell her you will come tuck her in and give her a kiss when you return. Leave and don't look back. If she is very young, she may, like most very young children, throw a temper tantrum to keep you there. Don't let it get to you, and don't turn back.

Chapter 14

You, Your Child, and the School

I see the mind of the 5 year old as a volcano with two
vents: destructiveness and creativeness.

— Sylvia Ashton-Warner

Our attention is so riveted by every day's minor miracles that we frequently lose sight of major miracles in the making. The first pale green leaf, the first intimation of color on the emerging bud, so miraculous in themselves, concentrate our awareness and block out the real miracle to come, the luminous beauty of the full blown rose.

So, too, with our child. The first miraculous though barely intelligible words, the first amazing if faltering steps, sufficient miracles for today, block our vision of the potential educator or astronaut. Without constant attention the potential rose will give up and fade away. So, too, the potential of the child.

Think, then, of the school as your child's garden. You are the gardener. Or, if you prefer, think of her school as an assembly line. You are the assembly-line manager. No responsible gardener, no responsible manager, would walk away saying, "I'll pick her up after you finish processing her." You are an essential component of the process.

For several years, a third of your child's life will center on school and school-related activities, which will largely determine her career; her social, political, and economic status; the kind of friends she will make; the kind of life she will live; the kind of person she will be; and her capacity for good in tomorrow's world. As a credentialed secondary education teacher, I believe that taking an interest in her schooling is taking an interest in her future.

You can effectively fulfill your parental responsibility during these strategic years by becoming part of the parent-student-school triangle.

FIND THE RIGHT SCHOOL

Check Out Official Records

College and university libraries (especially those that focus on teacher education) and public libraries (especially large city and county libraries) are mines of information. Ask the reference librarian where you can find reports on school rankings and reports on individual schools.

Check out the school's crime and safety record, too. Ask the police department how a particular school's crime record compares with other schools, and ask the fire department and the environmental people about its safety conditions.

Don't Confuse Class Size with Quality of Education

Radio and television chatter can mislead you about the importance of small classes. Your child can be as well educated in a class of thirty-seven as in a class of seven.

Our distinguished colleges and universities provide unsurpassed education in classes numbering in the hundreds. In grade school, as in grad school, quality depends not on the number of ears listening but on the overall competence of the educational network: teachers, teachers' aides, discipline, administration, budget, and curriculum.

Take a Practical Approach to the Money Issue

Keep an open mind on school selection. Setting your heart on a particular school can entrap you into a "shut up or put up" dilemma. Let me tell you what happened to me.

My daughter finished kindergarten at a parochial school, and I assumed she would routinely move on to first grade there. I was wrong; her mother informed me she would keep her there only if I paid the tuition. This, on top of the substantial monthly support I provided, was unreasonable. So I took a stand.

Public schools had given us and our friends a solid educational foundation, and I was confident they could do the same for our daughter. A thorough investigation of local schools confirmed my opinion; they offered excellent educational opportunities. Armed with this information and with a firm belief that a public school education would not jeopardize my child's future, I refused to pay the tuition.

As it turned out, my former spouse sent our daughter to parochial school anyway. But I am still convinced that we have equally excellent public schools. My former spouse made quite a point of telling me that her father had to defray part of the tuition; she sounded quite martyred, more concerned about her sacrifice than about any possible advantage to her daughter. Examine all alternatives before you succumb to blackmail. In education, as in life generally, the highest price does not guarantee the highest value.

Talk with Other Parents

Parents of children attending a school are your best source of information, and the PTA is the easiest place to contact them. The more parents you talk with, the clearer picture you'll receive.

Ask pertinent questions:

▷ How long have your children been in the school?
▷ How do they feel about the school?
▷ What kind of progress are they making?
▷ Do they have any complaints? Problems?
▷ Is parental involvement encouraged or resisted?
▷ What, if any, drug, alcohol, violence, discipline, or morale problems exist?

About the class your child will be in ask:

▷ Is the teacher effective? Supportive? Good at dealing with children?
▷ Are assignments and expectations age-related, sufficiently stringent to motivate the children without overburdening them?

Talk with the School Principal

Ask:

▷ Which of your programs would address my child's age and needs?
▷ What is your view of parental involvement?
▷ What, in your opinion, is the divorced parent's role in the school structure?
▷ Do you think this is the right school for my child?

Visit the School

Get a feel for the physical plant, for the attitude and conduct of students and staff. Look for signs of major discipline problems that could indicate a school out of control. Talk, if you get the chance, with students. Find out what they think about the school, its teachers, its programs, and its activities. Check the extracurricular activities. Are they adequate? Appropriate for your child?

PARTICIPATE IN YOUR CHILD'S SCHOOL PROGRESS

Eliminate the Cultural Lag

You may recall having heard the term "Cultural Lag" in some sociology class. It means, of course, the period during which a society's thinking lags behind changes in its actions, a period between the time people act in a new way and the time their thoughts catch up with their new actions. We are now in the last phases of the cultural lag created by our Father's Equal Parenting Movement. Until the lag ends, our position requires sensitive handling, nowhere more than in dealing with school personnel whose ideas haven't yet caught up with their actions.

The problem is merely that you are not always expected. Some school personnel still expect the mother, and here comes the father. Give them time to change gears. Suppose you go to see a man about a problem. Naturally, you enter his office with a mental picture of him sitting at his desk. But no. It's his wife. Or suppose you drop your car off at the service station. Expect to see a male mechanic, don't you? But what do we have here, a woman in heavy mechanic's overalls, wrench in one hand, competently throwing back the hood of your car with the other hand? Need time to get used to the idea? So do some members of the school staff. Smile. Be patient. Time will take care of it.

What to Tell the School About You

Tell the teachers and the school everything they need to know to do their job effectively and nothing more. Only you can determine exactly what they need to know. In general, you should give them facts about your divorce and your child's response to it, so they can be alert to her needs and let you know if any unusual divorce-related behavioral or emotional problems develop in the classroom.

The information they need does not include long, dreary accounts of pre-separation altercations and name-calling. (Don't give in to the post-divorce I-need-to-explain-everything syndrome. Respect the teacher's time; save the "True Stories" for the psychologist.) Nor does it entail an obligation to answer questions arising from personal curiosity rather than professional interest, or to accept unsolicited advice.

Discourage such questions and advice, but don't get indignant. Don't entangle yourself in complicated protestations. Just cool it. Body language can sometimes do the trick: a pause in the conversation, a slight frown, a mildly puzzled expression indicating you don't believe you heard correctly, a barely perceptible stiffening and leaning back in the chair, in short a snub, the way English royalty responds to unseemly questions. That's one way to handle it.

Here's another: Have handy a few standard expressions, appropriate to this specific situation, the kind travelers use in foreign countries. "I'm really not comfortable discussing it." "I would prefer not to talk about it right now." "I don't want to take up your time with personal details that don't shed any light on my daughter's situation." "That's nice of you to suggest, but I'm afraid it wouldn't fit in with our present arrangements."

Accept the Responsibility and its Demands

Like most divorced fathers, you were probably accustomed to seeing your child's mother take care of school-related chores, limiting your effort pretty much to sitting back and listening to a summary report.

Things have changed. It's time for you to dust off your hands and do some pick and shovel work. It will be grueling; you'll find it difficult at first, squeezing this new responsibility into your life. But once you get the knack, you'll enjoy it. Meanwhile, concentrate on its importance to your child, and keep moving.

Get All the Tools the Teacher Can Supply

As soon as Taryn registered for school, I wrote her teacher, combining a request for help with an offer of assistance. I told her that, despite my divorce from Taryn's mother, I shared equal responsibility for raising our daughter, that I did not want my child to grow up thinking of me as a stranger who paid the expenses and sent presents on holidays. I wanted to participate in her childhood years. In short, I wanted to be a real father.

I told her I needed direct information from the school because I could not depend on my former spouse to pass it on to me, and I asked her to keep me informed. Then I volunteered to help in the classroom or after school, as they needed and as my schedule permitted. (More about this below in "Beyond the Classroom.") When my former spouse heard about this letter, she protested that now they would know she was divorced. You can't win 'em all.

Let me recommend, even if you don't have time to give to the school, that you write the teacher explaining your situation and asking that she keep you fully informed about your child's activity and progress. It gets the information in her hands before she's bogged down with school start-up activity.

Before school opens, list the feedback you will need. Shortly after the first day, make an appointment with the teacher. When you meet, reinforce your request. Mention again, briefly, that you share equal responsibility with your child's mother for your child's educational development, and that this responsibility will necessitate your being aware of every aspect of the child's progress.

Be specific. This point must be made, and made clearly. Don't speak in generalities, name items such as report cards, newsletters, notices of school activities, and parent conferences. Ascertain what, exactly, the teacher can supply; who can provide the remainder; what, if any, additional resources the teacher can suggest.

If You Don't Get Action, Pursue It

The teacher can get snowed under, or your request can slip her mind. Whatever the reason, keep your cool. This is your chance to favorably impress one of the most important people in your child's life, your opportunity to demonstrate one of civilization's most polished achievements, the ability to conduct yourself with grace under pressure. Teachers are probably today's most stressed professionals; they don't need you acting like Attila the Hun.

The Next Step is the Principal's Office

This step is usually unnecessary because most teachers cooperate. But if they don't, you can't afford to drop it. Explain your problem briefly to the principal, and solicit his help in solving it.

Enlist the Aid of the School Secretary

The school secretary is at the hub of all school activity, and she can unravel most administrative tangles. To establish your need for information, again, briefly explain that you share equal parenting responsibility with your child's mother.

Ask her to: 1) Enter your name on the Class Roster of Parents or the Central School Information Card, whichever the school maintains for your child. (Give her all standard and emergency data the school keeps on file, including your home and business addresses, then ask what else she needs.) 2) Arrange to have a copy of all notices (especially report cards and parent conferences) mailed to your home as well as to the home of your former wife. 3) Advise you, as well as your former wife, of anything that affects your child, her activities, her welfare, or her education. Ask her what action, if any, you can take to facilitate compliance with your requests, such as providing self-addressed stamped envelopes.

BEYOND THE CLASSROOM

Don't Use the School as a Babysitting Service

You and I both know parents to whom a child is a frustrating burden, a limitation on freedom, an impediment to action. The school, to them, is part of a babysitting network, the main purpose of which is to take the kid off their hands and out of their hair. Every morning they impatiently drop the child off at the school parking lot; pick her up after school and drop her off at the curb of a day care facility; pick her up from there and plunge her into the hands of an overnight babysitter so they can entertain out-of-town buyers who don't like kids. These are the parents most prone to whine about parental responsibility, the parents who consider themselves, beyond all others, the best parents on the block.

Exaggerated? Perhaps, slightly. But it's true, in spirit, of parents who want the best for their children, but don't want to do anything about achieving it, like the citizen who wants good government but doesn't vote.

Try to arrange your visitation schedule so you can either drop your child off at school or pick her up after school, or better yet, both. It will add a bright note to your day and to your child's day. It will give a you a look at what's going on at the school and a chance to see her playmates.

Respect Your Child's School

Your attitude toward education will, to a large extent, shape your child's attitude toward education. And your child's attitude toward education will, to a large extent, shape her future.

Sometimes your influence is intentional when, for example, you talk with her about how a teacher fills children's minds with knowledge so they can grow up and make the world a better place, and you look into her wide Christmas-expectant eyes, you know you are opening up space in her brain where positive thoughts about learning can take root and grow.

But sometimes you teach your child to dislike school without even knowing it. This is expressly true of parents who had bad school experiences themselves or who think education is silly. They convey negative impressions wordlessly, by a shrug, a grimace, a tone of voice, or just plain lack of interest when the child talks about school. If this sounds like you, be aware of what you are doing. Don't cut her off before she gets started; give her a chance to experience education firsthand and make up her own mind if it's right for her.

There will be times when you think the school is mixed up or the teacher is dumb. And you may be right. Tell the school. Tell the teacher. But don't tell your child. You and the school and the teacher can patch it up and move on. But your child will sponge it up and remember. Then you'll wonder why she doesn't listen to you when you tell her to listen to her teachers.

Encourage her to respect her teachers. In truth, most of them deserve respect. Discourage her from complaining or criticizing. More importantly, set an example by being respectful yourself.

Attend School Functions

Attend school functions such as Parents Night, the Halloween Parade, Christmas Play, Annual Picnic, or student art shows.

Go to your child's music recitals, swimming meets, dance performances, and soccer games. Don't let your former wife's attendance scare you into staying away. Both of you can and should support your child's efforts. Success is empty if the people you love do not witness it and celebrate it with you. Focus on your child, support her in her efforts and in her achievements.

Volunteer to Help at the School

Volunteer to help the teachers or coaches. If something such as school band, swim team, or coaching particularly interests you, let them know. If you can't think of anything specific, just volunteer. Ask how you can help. In these tight-budget days, every school needs volunteers and they have a list of jobs backed up and waiting.

I work at the school and occasionally drive on field trips. Being around the children adds another dimension to my life, and a special closeness to Taryn and me, and I have developed a cooperative and mutually supportive relationship with the school personnel.

Tell them about any special skills or talents you may have; they can make use of anything. For instance, when I mentioned that I am a member of the Society of American Magicians, one of Taryn's teachers invited me to put on a demonstration for the children. I taught Taryn a few simple tricks, and the two of us presented a magic show at her school Christmas party. I have seen some truly great magic performances, and I have given some fairly good ones myself, but, in my mind, none are as wondrous as the Prestidigitation Act presented by Hill (Taryn) and Hill (Jerry) for the amazement and edification of Taryn's kindergarten class.

How to Use Homework to Help Your Child

Your child's homework can be an exciting adventure that instills an enduring and rewarding love of scholarship, or it can be a dreary task that embeds a lifelong resistance to learning. Now is the moment, and you are the person, to shape your child's future.

HOMEWORK TIME: "Time," the legal phrase goes, "is of the essence," and nowhere is it more essential than in homework. The first step is to establish when homework will be done. Negotiate with your child to fix an agreeable time and dedicate that period, every minute of it, to homework. Adherence to the schedule will build good study habits; deviation, for other than the most compelling reasons, will lead to procrastination and avoidance.

HOMEWORK PLACE: The second requirement is a quiet, physically comfortable area that is conducive to concentration. It can be as pretentious as a private den or as simple as a kitchen table, but it must be free from the distractions of television, radio, telephone, and the noise and activity of others playing or talking.

YOU: The third, and most fundamental, element is you; your awareness, your interest, and your guidance. Keep in mind that all children have homework; don't let your child tell you otherwise. If you have any questions, check with the teacher.

Take an active interest in what she's doing; read the assignments and discuss them enthusiastically. When she sees your interest, she will become interested, and this can lead to self-motivated achievement, the exhilaration of which can turn her into an object in motion, moving ahead under her own momentum.

Resist the temptation to do her work for her. Don't hang over her shoulder when she's working, but let her know where you'll be if she gets stuck. Your proper role is that of a guide. Encourage her to complete every project as well as she can. Then you, as a guide, can show her the path to a higher level of accomplishment. But first she must do her best on her own; otherwise she will never develop her mental muscles.

How to Use the Parent Conference to Help Your Child

Parent conferences are one-on-one meetings between the child's teacher and the child's parents or guardians. These conferences are confidential, and their purpose is threefold: 1) to provide an informal dialogue in an atmosphere where the people closest to the child can freely discuss their concerns, ask and answer questions, and make and receive suggestion; 2) to keep the parents abreast of the child's emotional, physical, and intellectual progress; 3) to provide assistance to parents in their efforts to sustain and forward the child's education.

Usually these conferences occur at the midpoint of each semester, allowing the first half-semester preceding the conference to observe and measure the child's progress, and the second half, following the conference, to take corrective or supportive action indicated by the conference findings. This is the parent's best and virtually only opportunity to ask direct, specific questions, and to learn and question the teacher's personal evaluation.

Many teachers will schedule a separate conference for each divorced parent. But if you and your former wife can tolerate the tension, it works out better if both of you meet with the teacher at the same time. Both of you will hear the same words at the same time; this should decrease arguments about what was said and what recommendations were made.

After the conference, both parents, for the sake of the child, should set aside their personal differences long enough to sit down and discuss the conference objectively, and decide what action to take.

How to Use the Report Card to Help Your Child

When you receive a report card, discuss it with your child. It is true that your former spouse also receives a copy of the report; it is also true that she has probably reviewed it with the child. That doesn't matter; it doesn't mean that you don't have to talk about it. You must create your own relationship and your own dialogue with your child; you must share your feelings.

The report card is to a child what the financial statement is to her parents; it's the bottom line document that determines her economic, social, and political status within her family and peer groups and, in the upper grades, it becomes her ticket for admission to honors high schools. So you don't have to lean on her about the importance of her report card; kids catch on pretty quick.

But you do have to work with her to turn around a bad report or to encourage a good report. So let's look first at the bad report. Assuming that your child, like my child and like most children, is pretty much down on herself already, knowing that she has disappointed you. Let her know that you love her, and that you don't judge her worth on the basis of the report card.

Let her know that you are deeply concerned about her report card, but don't pounce on her. She's discouraged enough already, and if you start screaming she will feel like an ax murderer, beyond redemption. She needs kind words and some appreciation to restore her confidence and give her the courage to try to pull her grades up.

"I'm pleased with most of your grades. You're doing a great job in _____ and _____. And an A in _____!"

Now, on to the problems.

"Let's look at algebra and English and see what the problems are so we can work on them."

Take a positive attitude. Approach every problem and every poor grade as a puzzle, a puzzle to be solved by you and your child. Encourage more study time, limit TV and after-school activities, if necessary. Set up special tutoring, if required. On the tough problems, meet with the teacher and your child to discuss ways and means.

If the report, especially the citizenship and socialization areas, indicates discipline or emotional irregularities, pay attention. Head-in-the-sand ostrich behavior won't do; Atlantic City doesn't hold enough sand to make these problems go away. That's your job. Try to find the cause. Are peer pressures turning your child against school? Are divorce-related problems destabilizing her? Is a faulty diet affecting her moods and behavior?

And now a few words about how to handle a good report. This, essentially, is not a difficult job. Something will come to mind naturally, I'm sure. Throw your hat up to the ceiling and catch it again? Throw your child up to the ceiling and catch her again? Buy her a yacht? Almost any little thing like that, just a token of your pleasure, will do.

Extend Her Horizons to Libraries, Museums, and Other Lovely Places

When your child is old enough to talk and walk, she's old enough to enjoy visiting libraries and museums. Keep visits brief and lively. Show that you enjoy being there. Your enthusiasm can ignite hers and these huge facilities will become familiar. She will be comfortable in them the rest of her life. Libraries and museums frequently feel alien to children who have to wait until they are taken there on school field trips; these children miss a great deal.

LIBRARIES: Show her how the library operates. Take her to the Children's Room, and show her the picture books, and how certain types of books are grouped together. Go with her to the story reading hours. Show her how the computer searches for a book, and let her have a try at the computer herself.

ART MUSEUMS AND GALLERIES: The more dazzling the colors the better. It's not important that she learn to distinguish a Mondrian from a Mickey Mouse; it's only important that she learn that art can be joyous.

If you are fortunate enough to be near a museum that designs scientific demonstrations to enthrall a child, such as San Francisco's world-acclaimed Exploratorium, she will fall forever in love with science. Lacking the Exploratorium, most any local museum will do. History and natural history museums will open her eyes to a past as adventure-packed as tomorrow's science fiction.

ZOOS, PARKS, AND SCHOOLS: No need to add zoos and parks to your "list of places to see." All parents know that your child will drag you there. But what about schools? Stupid, you say? Take a kid to look at schools? But consider: many colleges and universities are truly lovely. Few places can match them for elegance of architecture, scope and beauty of landscape, and the vibrant and orderly peace of intellectual activity. Years from now, the memory of walking with you amid towering grey gothic buildings on a snowy winter afternoon may well sustain your child's educational aspirations.

Chapter 15

The Miracle of Love: Dating and Remarriage

All you need is love/Love is all you need.

— John Lennon

We talked earlier about the need for good judgment in the period immediately after the divorce. Your friendships with women were, at that time, relatively superficial relations between two adults with the common objective of finding pleasant companionship. Now that your equilibrium has stabilized somewhat, you and your child are reunited, and your new living quarters are working smoothly, you will, attractive gentleman that you are, be meeting many bewitching ladies.

But the introduction of your child into the picture will complicate romantic affairs. Simple relationships will shift into complex webs of distinct but interlocking relations between 1) your child and you; 2) you and your loved one; 3) your child and your loved one; all of which will be further compounded by a new and wide disparity of ages and goals.

DATING

Dating presents special, but surmountable, difficulties.

Your child must learn to relinquish her sole ownership of you. Your dates, especially those who do not themselves have the responsibility of children, must adjust their picture of you as the dashing free-spirited bachelor to the more realistic father-of-child with heavy responsibility, and they must face the necessity of sharing your love with your child.

You must help them both achieve these not inconsiderable emotional tasks. Instability will further complicate the situations, the introduction of each new date setting off a new imbalance and requiring a new stabilization.

On the plus side of dating, remember, it doesn't last forever.

One day you'll find the lady you want to date for the rest of your life. Of course, that will involve other complications. Life is a dazzling river with rapids all the way. Some rapids are exciting; others, just plain rough and dangerous. We'll discuss the latter shortly.

In the meantime, dating will be tumultuous. You and your child will both make mistakes, and the mistakes will teach you to better understand yourselves, to share loved ones with others, and to love others — abilities that will pay off handsomely when you both form a permanent association with that special lady who will, in a sunny tomorrow, brighten both your lives.

Look Through Your Child's Eyes

Children, because they are unable to cope with life alone, are easily threatened by the appearance of a new love-object in the family such as a new baby or even a new pet. Our children, who have personally experienced the separation and fear of separation attending divorce, are doubly threatened.

Try to put yourself in your child's position; try to stand in her shoes with a child's dependence and a child's fears; look through her eyes. This is especially important when you are dating. With the end of a relationship, she will think all danger has ended, only to be faced with the beginning of new relations and new dangers.

Try to understand that your child may feel alone, unloved, and rejected; she may resent you because she feels you have deserted her for your new interest.

Comfort her. Reassure her. Tell her of your inexhaustible love for her. When you spend time with her, be there with her mentally as well as physically; nothing will banish her fears as quickly.

Try to understand that your child may resent your dates because she fears they will rob her of your love. Tell her that no one will ever take her very special place in your heart. Tell her that, just as she needs friends of her own age, you need friends of your age, but it's a different kind of love, just as her love for you is different from her love for her friends.

Look through Your Date's Eyes

As a father, you have dedicated part of yourself, of your time, your emotion, and your money to your child. This is a fact of life that distinguishes you from a no-other-strings lover. Different women, as you have probably noted, respond differently to this fact.

Some women consider any expenditure of emotion or money on others as a deduction from what is rightly due them. Some look on the child as an irksome restriction on the time you should spend with them. Some give up before they start, afraid to contest such a love as you have for your child, certain there is no place for them in so full a heart. So much for them. Nice people, pleasant dates, but not a divorced father's ideal friend.

Some women feel that — in this self-centered day of fragile, fleeting relationships — a love such as yours for your child is one of the very few sure indicators of a strong and loving character. Some look upon it as an opportunity to demonstrate the depth of their love by sharing your joys, your burdens, and your love. And many come to love the child as deeply as you do. (Not to be confused with those who "just adore the child, whatshername" to win brownie points from you.)

When you find such a jewel, treasure her. Tell her every day in different ways, of your love. Even the most loving, devoted, and generous heart needs reassurance.

To Date or Not to Date

You should not date because:
▷ Your friends or your mother think you should
▷ It would be nice to have a housekeeper
▷ You want to spite your former wife
▷ You want a surrogate mother or role model for your child
▷ You need to have someone, anyone, around.

You should not let your child be a determining factor. Know what you want, and make your own decisions.

You should date because:
▷ You want to date
▷ It would make your life happier and more complete
▷ You have met someone you particularly like.

You may feel, now or in the future, that you owe your main loyalty to your child. She is just a child, and your date will understand. This is true only as it applies to your basic commitments to your child. You must not let others infringe on the rights of your child, nor let your child infringe on the rights of others.

Tantrums as You Leave for a Date

Children commonly throw tantrums just as you start out the door. Jealousy or fear of losing you frequently activates a last-ditch stand to keep you home. It is to be expected, but it is not to be encouraged. Surrendering to manipulation encourages further manipulation.

Do not react emotionally. Sit with your child, reassure her that you love her and that when you come home you will check on her, tuck her in, and kiss her goodnight. Turn her over to the babysitter, and walk out the door. Wave back, but don't be coerced into going back.

When Your Babysitter Cancels

You have planned a special date, your babysitter cancels, and you can't locate a substitute. What now?

Bring your date home, or the two of you take the child to a place that will work for all three. Most of the nice people you know will willingly accommodate such an emergency. If the lady in question finds it too disagreeable, you're a very lucky man to find that out right now.

When Your Conversation With Your Date Revolves Around Children

You may find your conversation pivoting around your children, and if your date has children, around her children. This sometimes happens because dating, especially a first date, no matter your age, can be awkward; because you've been married so long, you've forgotten how to talk about anything but children; or because your interest is monopolized by your children.

If you're the only one hung up on the subject, discreetly check your watch, and make an agreement with yourself that you'll talk about other subjects for at least an hour. If it's both of you, set a pact with her for an hour.

Otherwise, the sum total of your knowledge about her as the evening ends will be that she's well informed about your children. Get to know her; if the evening leads anywhere, there will be lots of time to talk about children. Talk about her, about her interests, her work, her goals and aspirations, her travels. It has been said many times, by many wits, that nothing impresses others with your intelligence as quickly as asking them questions about themselves. Questions, not answers, get a relationship off on a good footing.

If you are one of those people who, correctly or incorrectly, think yourself a poor conversationalist, read a few books on how to hold a conversation. Your bookseller or librarian can point them out to you.

Many of these books are funny and reader-friendly; you can zip right through them. They will explain how to get a conversation off the ground by asking questions, and how to keep it aloft by following up on the answers. Easy as flying a kite. You'll never again find yourself at a loss in conversation.

When You Can't Wait to Get Home to the Kids

Some fathers find themselves on a date and then they can't wait to get home and cook dinner for the kids, or they call home every half hour "to find out how they're doing." If you didn't make adequate arrangements before you left, you should not be here. If you did make adequate arrangements, including leaving the telephone number where you can be reached, your children are fine. Put that telephone down. Frequent calls only upset the children and the babysitter.

The real question is, why are you here in the first place? You are demonstrably ill at ease. And can you imagine your date? She probably thinks she's dining with an on-duty security guard.

If you don't want to date, stay home with the children. Or go out to dinner with the children. Or bring the children with you on the date. That's fine. Just don't take up the lady's time and act as though she's not there.

When Your Date Suggests You Spend the Night

Don't leave the children with a babysitter overnight unless there's an absolute emergency. Children want to know that you are home with them.

If this is something you want to do, and if you feel morally comfortable with it, ask for a raincheck, and explain your reasons. A mumbled, "Some other time, maybe," sounds too much like a brush-off, and she may wish she had held her tongue.

When it's Difficult to Share Your Child's Time

Many fathers, especially those of us who had to fight for time with our children, are reluctant to share them with other people. We treat friends, especially women friends, as visitors, promoting an artificially formal distance between them and our children, as if to protect our children from attachments to others. Or perhaps to protect ourselves from losing the children, or to defend the family from outside invasion.

Whatever the motive, it is unfair to everyone. A friend should be welcomed for all to enjoy, and to enrich the family circle. Coffee cups and napkins in the living room are acceptable on a first visit, if you can't live without token formality, and if you make it clear that the "visitor act" ends with the first visit. After that, let's include everyone in family activities, from games and decisions to candy making. It's important and exciting for your children to socialize with adults, if they don't always have to treat them like visitors.

Getting Your Children and Your Dates Together

No child will like every adult, and no adult will like every child, and no amount of meddling will alter that fact. But you will never know which is which unless they spend some time together. You, yourself, can't tell from across the street whether you like a person, but spend some time with him and you'll decide quickly. First impressions are not necessarily true or lasting, but we live life a day at a time.

Bring children and adults together in an easy, casual atmosphere, and let them work out their own relationships at their own tempo.

The setting is important and your options are limitless — the zoo, a boat trip, bowling, fishing, baseball and football games, afternoon theater, art galleries, bird watching, concerts in the park, picnics at the beach, hiking. Select the ones in which all parties will be sufficiently interested to bring out their personalities, but not so obsessively absorbed as to exclude awareness of other people.

Repress the urge to tell the adults how wonderful the children are, and vice versa. Resist even more strenuously the urge to choreograph every step. Leave it alone. They don't need a ringmaster.

When There's No Free Time at Home

When you feel you never have time for yourself, time to talk to friends or dates on the telephone, or just time to sit and think; when life begins to crowd you and you think your children are making unreasonable demands; when you seem to spend all your time taking care of them — give yourself some space.

Block out specific periods of time and post them on the refrigerator. Tell your children that this is your free time, that you are not to be interrupted unless it is an emergency. If necessary, hang a sign on your doorknob: "Daddy's free time. Do not disturb."

LOVE

From Dating Many to Loving One

If you have, as suggested in the preceding pages, included your dates in family activities changing from dating many to loving one will present fewer difficulties. This is not to say it will present no difficulties.

The difficulties to which you must address yourself arise out of fear and are, in the full-blown form we see today, a phenomenon of our accelerating divorce rate. 1) The child, because she is dependent upon her father's protection, fears a loss of the love that could result in a loss of comfort, protection, and security. 2) The lady, because she makes a full commitment of her love, fears that the father's love, previously committed to his child, may leave little room for her.

These two areas of fear are inextricably interwoven in the complex relationship between you, your child, and your lady which we discussed earlier. For clarity, however, we'll discuss them as if they can be separated.

Understand Your Child's Insecurity

If your child and your lady have had an opportunity to become acquainted, they can have formed the beginnings of a loving family-bond between them.

When, however, you singled the lady out as your one love, you may have jarred the emerging relationship. Up to this point, your child, holding stage center in your heart and in your home, saw the lady as a visitor. Now the visitor has suddenly turned into an adult with equal, if not greater, claim on your love. And in the mind of a young child — coping with the uncertainties of this nuclear age, recuperating from the emotional bruises of a broken home, burdened with an instinctive multi-million-year species-specific terror of childhood's insecurity — fear stirs.

Keep your eye on this situation. Be alert for unusual behavior or danger signs. Keep in touch with the child's feelings by casual references that will invite her to express her feelings without pressuring her to do so. Your lady herself, if she is sufficiently sure of your love, may be your greatest ally in observing, analyzing, and dealing with these problems.

In the absence of any obvious discomfort on either side, encourage your lady and your child to spend some time alone so they can get to know each other better. Suggest things like shopping, walking, bike riding, or flying kites in the park. Don't confuse this activity with babysitting. Don't turn your child over because you want to be free to do something else, but rather for the positive reason that you want your two loves to know and, if possible, love each other.

Be prepared for the possibility that increased closeness between the lady and the child may develop latent conflicts that have been camouflaged by the previous, and more formal, relationship of child and visitor.

More subtle reasons than considered above may motivate your child's rejection of a woman in the house. For example, many children treasure an obscure hope, generally unexamined and unexpressed, that the mother and father will remarry, the three of you will live together again, and everything will be just like it was before the divorce. While this hope lives, the child may think your new love is causing the final break between you and her mother, and she will resent the woman as the cause of this finality. The child who accepted a series of visitors may refuse to accept the woman you love.

If you encounter this particular problem:

1) Assure your child that you do understand her feelings.

2) Tell her that you are not, under any circumstances, going to get back together with her mother. The child cannot be at peace with your decision until she understands its absolute finality.

3) Assure her of the permanence of her place in your heart.

Sometimes, too, especially when a father lives alone, a child may gradually develop a feeling of exclusive ownership, and resent any adult who challenges her right of possession.

The Oedipus Complex, as discussed earlier, can intensify this problem in a young girl. Under its influence, she may think of herself as the lady of the house and feel very secure in her possession of her father's love. Any adult, especially a woman, becomes a rival for her father's love and her privileged position in his home.

The Best Medicine is Love

These and most other rivalries between your child and your loved one emanate from uncertainty about the strength and constancy of your love. The surest balm for uncertainty is reassurance. Provide honest explanations and reassurance. And lots of love.

And a last word: If you see any indication of pain that lasts too long or cuts too deep, don't make the mistake of thinking that the child will get over it, that it's just a matter of time. Too many young lives have been permanently scarred by unthinking and uninformed dismissal of their pain.

Call for an appointment with a child psychologist or child psychiatrist. They can frequently discover in an hour or two what you and I might never see.

You and Your Loved One

Today's divorced fathers have an ethical obligation to understand and, if possible, prevent the problems we create in the lives of the women who love us.

The first problem evolves from our society's traditional view of married love: two people who, forsaking all others, each putting the other ahead of everything and everyone in the world, take each other for better or worse, for richer or poorer, in sickness and in health. This high ideal has, unfortunately, been romanticized into a lacy valentine, frequently leading to expectations that a divorced father, who cannot forsake his child, cannot fulfill.

This is not to say that a divorced father cannot be an exemplary husband. As a famous poet said, "I could not love thee, dear so much, loved I not honor more." Any divorced father who beguiles a woman into marriage knowing that she does not understand this fact is, in my opinion, performing a dishonorable act and the marriage is, in spirit if not in law, fraudulent. Odds are high that he will soon return to the divorce court, all about him in pain, his life again in shambles.

Lack of communication, not fraud, is usually at the root of such tragedies. People in love frequently assume that everything is as they wish it to be, and investigate no further. After marriage they discover that, while they thought they were thinking alike, they were dreaming different and mutually exclusive dreams. After the marriage is the wrong time to find out.

Talk now. If she has no children and has never been responsible for a child's care (babysitting does not qualify as experience of this stature), your main obligation is to make sure she understands that:

1) A child is not a pretty toy you keep in a box most of the year and take out and dress daintily for the holidays.

2) A child is not a docile, submissive creature who will always love you and always do as you say.

3) A child is a contrary, difficult, puzzling individual requiring infinite care and attention, who will demand your love, tell you she hates you, and who will throw a tantrum or catch the measles and mess up your vacation plans.

4) A child is a surprising little person, full of imagination and chuckles and love, blossoming into full humanity right under your eyes.

You and your future wife do not have to, and never will, agree on everything, but you must share and support each other's goals. This is especially true in regard to your child.

That she accept your love for your child is as important as that your child accept your love for her.

The Question of Affection

The question will inevitably arise, should you or should you not show affection for your lady in front of your children. The answer is an unqualified yes.

Unlike other species, we have no instinctive pattern through which to express our love. So children must learn, and they learn largely through observing the adults around them. Socially acceptable expression of love and affection is one of the many things you teach your child through your actions. It is important that children see normal, healthy affection and love.

This leads to the question of just what constitutes appropriate expression in the presence of a child. We could get involved in a lot of specifics, but I find this rule-of-thumb more flexible and more useful: any display of affection that I would consider appropriate for a couple visiting my home is appropriate for me.

And that leads to the question, is it appropriate for your love and you to spend the night together at your home?

It is, of itself, not inappropriate, unless you let your bedroom door become a revolving door. Don't spring any surprises. Give your child time to know the lady, to understand that this one person is very, very special to you, and to gradually get used to the idea. When she does spend the night, don't try to hide the fact that she is there. Your children are smarter about these things than you realize.

How Long Should You Wait Before You Remarry?

Marriage counselors caution against remarrying before you regain your balance, and they generally agree that it can take a year, sometimes longer. Evidence of the validity of their opinion lies all about us every day. Marriages occurring shortly after a divorce almost invariably end in a second divorce.

Even at its least stormy, divorce severs one of man's deepest, most binding, most emotional ties. It is usually followed by grief akin to that created by the loss of a friend or a death in the family, disorienting us and shaking the foundations of our understanding.

Elisabeth Kubler-Ross, an authority on death and grieving, says that before we can accept death, we must pass through the four stages of grief: denial, anger, depression, and acceptance. The same is true of divorce.

Any remarriage, before completion of grief and coming to terms with the past, is a marriage based on illusion. It can end easily in tragedy — for you, your wife, and your child.

"To love forever," a very wise person once observed, "can never be a sincere promise. It can only be a sincere hope." Until you free yourself of the past, it cannot even be a sincere hope. It can only be a sincere illusion.

When You Know You've Found Your True Love

To know anything is to understand it through some rational system and, in this limited sense, you will never know you are in love. Honor, respect, admiration, happiness, physiology, devotion, these are aspects of love we can know. But even in today's cynical world, love is also magic and miracle, and these aspects we can neither know nor evaluate, we can only believe.

But don't let me discourage you, please. There are some pretty good indicators. You can be reasonably certain you are in love when:

> ▷ You have given yourself time to grieve and are looking forward optimistically to a new life.
> ▷ You don't compare your love to the wives of your friends, smug in your knowledge that they will be envious.

▷ You think of marrying her without even a gleeful sideways mental glance at the possibility of revenge on your
former wife.

▷ You want to spend the rest of your life with her.

▷ You want an ideal marriage, as defined by the noted
scholar and author Joseph Campbell, that transcends
you and your love and is based, not exclusively on your
commitments to each other, but to your individual
commitments to the relationship itself.

MARRIAGE

Children in the Wedding Ceremony

The wedding day is the bride's day, and the wedding ceremony
is the centerpiece of her day. Inclusion of anyone in the ceremony
should be her decision. If, to her, a wedding symbolizes the formation
of a spiritual bond between the bride and groom, she may feel that
the addition of family members would depreciate the symbolism. On
the other hand, if she thinks a marriage bonds the bride and groom
and all those family members whose lives will be affected then, by all
means, the children, sisters, brothers, aunts, and uncles — everyone.

Children on the Wedding Trip

Traditionally, the purpose of the wedding trip has been to permit the bride and groom to leave and make a definite break with their
former status, so they can return to the community to assume their
newly acquired and fully acknowledged status as a married couple.
But, again, it depends on the bride's wishes and her wishes will probably depend on her relationship with the children. If, as sometimes
happens, she would feel as lonesome and incomplete as you without
the children, by all means — a caravan.

Bride/Stepmother

Most little girls, playing with their dolls, dream of becoming
brides and mothers. But after reading Cinderella, few dream of becoming stepmothers. Stepmothers have bad press and bad role models. Yet every day new brides plunge in unprepared.

Some of the most treasured women I know overcame bad press,
bad role models, and inexperience to become great stepmothers. Almost to a woman, they admit they are not self made; they survived
with the love and support of their husbands.

Your bride's success as a stepmother depends largely on you, her husband, and on how, in the silent depths of your own mind, you view the role of stepmother. If you see her as a glorified housekeeper whose existence is justified by service to your child, or if you see her as a replacement for the child's mother, you will program a disaster. No woman worthy of the name will accept the first role or attempt the second.

If you see your wife primarily as an individual, your beloved bride, your lifetime companion and lover who supports your goals as you support hers, she can bring joy to your home as well as your heart. And she will probably also be a great stepmother.

Keep the Sparkle in Her Life

I know a man who works for the Department of Defense, and I think he's misplaced; he should be with the State Department. His work requires considerable travel and, one Mother's Day, he forgot to call, write, send flowers, anything; he just forgot. Next day, he called home. For five minutes he listened to the explosive ire of his fine Scotch lass who knew her rights. Silence, at last, on the line. Then he explained, "I'm sorry, my love, but I always think of you as a bride, not a mother."

Always think of your wife as a bride. Appeal to the bride in her, and you'll reach the wife and mother. Everything else will fall into place.

Keep the Sparkle in Your Sex Life

Sex after marriage can differ from your expectations. That doesn't mean it can't sparkle.

Arrange private time with her, time alone together that belongs exclusively to the two of you. Create romantic mornings — welcome the sunrise on a bicycle built for two or fly kites on a windy hillside. Afternoons stroll through a winery or an art gallery. Enjoy a picnic lunch by the lake side. In the evenings try theater, dinner, a night at the local hotel.

Create romantic evenings at home. Plan ahead: send her roses in the afternoon. Select her favorite wine. Light the candles. Dig out her favorite records. Install a good babysitter, with instructions that children are not to wander about. Cordon off part of the house for yourselves — off limits to everyone else. Pull the plug on the telephone. The television. The radio. You are the only two people on earth.

Stepmother and Children

Several questions will quickly arise about your new bride's relationship with your child. Now is the time to start thinking about them.

WHAT IS THE STEPMOTHER TO BE CALLED?

Has such an essentially trivial question ever spawned more family heartbreak? One of my colleagues has been at sword's point with his father and stepmother since their marriage three years ago. The sticking point is that, in deference to his mother's memory, he can't call another woman "mother." The word catches in his throat, and his father and stepmother interpret it as a deliberate and intentional insult to the stepmother. Such a tragedy! With so many alternatives, a family tears itself apart over one word.

The children should not be pressured to use any specific name, nor should the stepmother be pressured to accept any. The stepmother should have veto authority over any name she dislikes. But if everyone agrees, the children could propose names from which the stepmother can select one, or the stepmother could propose and the children select.

DOES THE STEPMOTHER REPLACE THE MOTHER?

No. The biological mother remains the mother; her relationship to the child is unique. It cannot be challenged, shared, or changed. Attempting to alter it is a waste of energy, as futile as trying to reverse the forces of nature.

WHAT IS THE STEPMOTHER'S ROLE?

The stepmother is primarily a wife, the lady of the house, and the leading lady in her husband's life. She is a stepmother only as a consequence of being a wife.

There is no standard position description. The role varies from family to family, and is determined largely by the degree of the wife's love, commitment, and capability.

Formulating Discipline

You and your wife should jointly arrive at a set of carefully thought out, consistent, fair, and enforceable rules applicable to the circumstances, activities, and ages of the children. The rules should then be presented at a family meeting, after which open discussion, suggestions, questions, and objections should be welcomed. Really welcomed. Don't ask for suggestions and glare at the first person who opens his mouth.

Consider all responses and, if possible, accommodate them. If you can't, explain why. Recognize each suggestion, with applicable comments on intelligent, workable, or practical ideas.

Before the meeting ends, you should establish the lines of

authority. Make it clear that you are still the final authority, just as you were before the marriage, but there are certain areas in which the children must do as the stepmother says.

Firm and sensitive handling of the authority question now can avert rebellion. Your marriage and the delegation of disciplinary authority are two convergent flash points just begging to be ignited. It's a natural setup for the opening shot of the war, "You can't tell me what to do. You're not my mother." Save your bride from that. Invest her with full, clearly defined, authority, such as "in my absence" or "in regard to schoolwork" or "when you are crossing the street."

Call for a discussion period after the announcements. Dig right in and answer every question fully. Any haziness and the children will be as irritated as you and I are when we get double and conflicting bills on a charge card, and can't figure which is right.

Maintaining Discipline

Once the framework of authority has been set in place, your wife can progressively augment the depth and scope of her authority as her bond with the children matures and strengthens.

From here on, the two of you should work out decisions in private away from the children, and then meet with the children together to announce and discuss them. Support each other, and present a consistent and united front.

Stepmother vs Former Spouse

Here's another flash point. Just because your former wife may have been delighted to get rid of you, don't assume that she's delighted to see someone else get you.

Since the divorce, your former wife has created a new world for herself, and her relationship with you is a major part of it. Your marriage, by changing that relationship, can knock her little world off its axis. Be alert for troublesome attacks, especially attacks on your new wife.

A divorced woman may find the singles world less promising than promised, and toy with the idea of remarrying her former husband. His marriage cuts off her possibility of retreat.

If she's an egomaniac, she may view your happiness as a personal insult. I once worked with a sadistically vain woman who always spoke of her former husband as "my late husband." When I commented that I hadn't realized she was a widow, she replied, "Oh, I'm not. I call him 'my late husband' because I'm sure that being divorced from me is a kind of death." Remarriage of her "late" husband could seriously damage this woman's self-image.

The apprehensions of a divorced mother also extend to how your marriage may affect her child. There is the matter of custody; courts look more favorably on a father's requests when he remarries and establishes a home. And alienation of affection; sharing her child's time with another woman is scary. Many children have become closer to their stepmothers than their mothers. And spousal or child support; new wives have been known to effect a negative cash-flow in such arrangements. And the child's "rights": new children of a new marriage have been known to push children of a first marriage out of a father's life and estate.

Some Ambush Techniques

A fearful or bitter former wife will use any tool at hand, including her child, to bedevil your wife. She may brainwash the child until she instills discourtesy, rebellion, and hate. Or she may use the child to keep both of you on edge in the hope of sowing discord. She may sabotage plans, upset schedules, fail to be there when you go to pick the child up, fabricate reasons the child cannot go, or not have the child ready at the right time.

She may encourage her boyfriend to confront, insult, slight, or embarrass your wife. She may, herself, directly attack your wife. And she may try to create strife between the two of you by a sudden show of affection for you.

Some Anti-Ambush Techniques

You and your wife should sit down together and list all of the situations under which she comes in contact with your former wife. Then systematically cut these down to an absolute minimum.

Do not ask your wife to pick the child up or return her. The picture of this woman taking the child away from her home may confirm the mother's most primitive fears and bring down irrational abuse on your wife. I know from experience that it feels great to turn this job over to someone else; make it someone other than your wife. Pick the child up yourself or make other arrangements.

Do not allow your child to make negative comments about your wife.

Try to avoid aggravating your former spouse. Continue to live up to your commitments. Be on time. Pay on time. Don't be goaded into verbal combat. And don't boast about your wife, or throw her in the face of your former spouse.

You and Your Child

The arrival of a new stepmother, no matter how kind and loving and well-intentioned, troubles a child. It brings change and rumbles of more change, a new family, a new home, possibly new brothers and sisters. Younger children may accept the stepmother more easily than adolescents but all, regardless of age, will undergo substantial stress. Until this stress runs its course and settles down, a child may be emotionally incapable of forming a deep attachment to anyone, including the stepmother.

Encourage open communication. Create opportunities for sharing of feelings and ideas at family meetings.

Don't look for a simplistic TV sitcom solution. Gathering people together under one roof does not immediately transform them into a family. Your job is not finished. Be patient. And surround your child with sensitive, loving support.

A MESSAGE TO THE STEPMOTHER

There are no shortcuts to love. Overindulgence, doing too much and giving too much, will not make your stepchildren love you, it will just make them greedy.

Invite the children to ask questions. Encourage them to talk about what's going on in their lives — their problems, complaints, jokes, demands, likes, dislikes, feelings, expectations, dreams, worries, fears.

Listen closely. Always acknowledge that you heard what they said. Then give yourself time to process the information before reacting. If you can listen and take time to think, you will react appropriately.

Be yourself. Give the children time to adjust to you. Let them help you. Invite them to bring their friends around. Be friendly. Be flexible.

Chapter 16

The Gift of Child-Centered Time

The more you love your children the more care you should take to neglect them occasionally. The web of affection can be drawn too tight.

— D. Sutten

CREATING CHILD-CENTERED TIME

The term child-centered time is fairly self-explanatory. No doubt you'll grasp the idea without any assistance from me. But just to be on the safe side — if you'll bear with me — child-centered time is the time a father spends in direct or indirect interaction with his child. Direct interaction, for the purposes of my definition, is face-to-face (personal) or voice-to-voice (telephone) closeness between father and child during which the child is aware that he commands the father's active attention. Indirect interaction is project-related closeness between father and child during joint participation in an activity during which the child is aware that the activity creates a common bond between him and his father.

Going Through the Motions is Not Child-Centered Time

When your child finishes telling you a riddle and looks up to see you gazing into space, your thoughts obviously centered elsewhere, that's not child-centered time.

When you're playing checkers and he has to keep reminding you, "It's your turn," that's not child-centered time.

When the two of you are putting his bicycle together, and you become so absorbed in the project he has to remind you of your three o'clock appointment, that's child-centered time.

And when you come home and ask him how his day went and how he feels, and you listen to his answers, and you care about what he says, that's child-centered time.

The Gift of Child-Centered Time

Child-centered time empowers you to create miracles in your child's life. With your attention, he will be more alert, more attentive, brighter, and happier. Recent studies report that, despite its value to the child, the average father spends no more than twenty minutes a week actively interacting with his children. These studies were apparently made with fathers in intact homes. I'll bet the average time would be higher for divorced fathers. We who have faced the possibility of losing contact with our children, value every minute more highly.

Child-centered hours, as many as possible, are the greatest gifts you can give your child. He'll remember them long after the bicycle is replaced by a Jaguar, and God granting him a long, long life, years from now he'll chuckle as he tells his cronies at the club what you said last week, and will quote you word for word.

THE VALUE OF A POSITIVE SELF-CONCEPT

According to Carl R. Rogers, founder of Non-directive Counseling, a person, by associating with others, develops a self-concept, a picture of himself, and then behaves in agreement with that picture. Rogers finds that people are strongly motivated toward positive change and growth; that, with proper encouragement, they tend to realize their potential; and that the more positive a person's self-concept, the more likely he is to succeed.

Positive Self-Concept Leads to High Self-Esteem

A child's high self-esteem, belief in himself and his capabilities, is an outgrowth of a positive self-concept or self-image. It enables him to achieve normal physical and emotional development, good personal relationships at home and at school, and a high level of scholarship; to develop independence, responsibility, and leadership; and to face change enthusiastically and accept challenge confidently.

Give Your Child a Head Start

In Chapter 2, we talked about how you could make your self-image work for you. This would be an excellent time to review that material with your child, and talk with him about his self-image. Give him a head start. Put him in control of his own self-image and thereby his life and success.

A child's picture of himself begins to develop when he is born and, according to most behavioral scientists, how he interprets the responses of the people around him during the next six or seven years sets the pattern of his self-concept and self-esteem.

Most children spend their early years with their parents who, as a consequence, have a heavy input into the child's opinion of himself and a heavy responsibility to make that opinion as positive as they can.

Don't give up if your child thinks himself a failure at, say, eight. That would be like a traveler continuing on the wrong road because he took a wrong turn. Social workers, psychologists, and psychiatrists are becoming increasingly effective in helping children rehabilitate the self-concept and raise the self-esteem. Never give up. But given the opportunity, help your child develop high self-esteem early; it will be easier on both of you.

Factors that Foster a Child's Self-Esteem

One of the most important factors is connection with, and approval from, the important people in his life, especially his parents. This is a sobering thought to a divorced father, whose connection with his child has been severely shaken during the divorce and post-divorce period.

It is also crucial that he feel good about what he is, what he has, what he has achieved. Identification with a group (family, neighborhood, team, club) has been identified as one of man's most primitive needs, dating from prehistoric times when men banded together for mutual protection. Fear of exclusion from the group, through disgrace, dishonor, business failure, is, to this day, one of man's deepest fears.

Help Your Child Strengthen His Self-Esteem

Play, kiss, hold, touch, hug, wrestle. Often. Affectionate physical contact is, to your child, a happy assurance of your presence and your love, a sure esteem raiser.

Smile. A lot. Your smile makes the world safe.

Show he's special by doing special things. Tag one day a month as This is Your Day. Cook his, not your, favorite dish; play his, not your, favorite card game.

Set an example of sound values and high integrity. Expose him to good role models in life and literature. Children unconsciously absorb the attitudes and behaviors of people in their lives — parents, family members, relatives, friends, teachers, and fictional characters.

Help him set attainable goals, and encourage him to take responsibility for decision-making.

Encourage him to do things on his own, work after school, prepare his own meals.

Encourage him to express his imagination and creativity. Your recognition of his personality enables him to perceive his unique potential.

Demonstrate your pride in his achievements. Praise him when he does well in school or weeds the garden. During long-term projects, give him positive feedback at each step along the way. Maximize praise. Minimize criticism.

Keep Your Own and Your Child's Self-Esteem in Good Repair

Your self-esteem, like your clothing, suffers everyday wear and tear; both require occasional mending. As you work on your child's self-esteem, check on your own. They are closely connected.

A parent with low self-esteem becomes fearful, loses self-confidence, is unable to communicate freely, and sees anything the child wants to do as a threat to the parent-child relationship. Such a parent, feeling unworthy of being loved, living in fear that a successful child will outgrow the need for a father, may unconsciously discourage the child's mental and emotional growth, and give him mixed messages about success.

Your child's self-esteem is not a one-time project. Like your car, it requires periodic checks and service. Give it at least as much time and attention as you give your car.

LETTING GO

The Parent-Child Relationship

The parent-child relationship is unique. You willingly and happily — in fact you fight for the right to — devote eighteen to twenty years to a child; make substantial investments of time, effort, money, and love; put her health, security, and welfare ahead of yours.

Then, on a day's notice, the child is an adult, and you must step back, withdraw your hands, speak as if to a casual acquaintance, ask no questions and offer no advice, in short, abandon a priceless property, the major investment of your life.

To act similarly in the business world would be to submit not only your good sense but your sanity to question. Imagine your banker's response if you were to voluntarily hand your business, representing a fraction of your investment in your child, over to a virtual stranger. Imagine what your associates would say if you labored for years to build an ideal home and when it was finished, you packed up, left graciously, and quit-claimed all rights. These, obviously, are not exact parallels, but they're pretty close.

There is something in the parent-child relationship that makes the investment joyous and the "letting go" possible — less possible for some than for others. And for us divorced fathers, who fought for every treasured day, it sometimes seems impossible. It is not. We can do it. Begin today.

Recognize that if you don't learn to let go now, she may not learn to let go later. It's all very well to say, "But she's only a child." That's like saying, "But she's only a doll." It sounds nice and safe — as though she is a static and unchanging object. She's about as static as an acorn doing its job of becoming an oak tree. She's busy on her job of becoming an adult, a doomed project if you isolate her from everyday experiences, decisions, and risks essential to her growth. When you release her to fly on her own, she must be ready to use her wings. Let her begin today.

Recognize that you must "let go" when she starts school and is no longer with you round the clock; when she finishes school and her career absorbs her attention; when she takes an assignment in Australia and all you see are postcards; when she becomes a parent herself and her children require from her the same investment you made.

From this day on, no matter the age of your child, life will demand one small "letting go" after another, and each "letting go" will permit her to move toward maturity, independence, and the ability to cope with the world. It's the price we pay for the privilege of being parents.

You're not letting go when:
- ▷ Your whole life revolves around your child
- ▷ You want to be with her every minute, and you want to be included in everything she does
- ▷ You have to get involved in every game she begins
- ▷ You worry if she walks out of the house to play in a safe, secure area
- ▷ You are constantly in and out of the house, to visit with her, make sure she is all right, hover, fuss, worry
- ▷ You try to control her life even when she is not with you
- ▷ You bring her late or pick her up early when she goes to a party or visits friends
- ▷ You want to do everything for her — you decide about meals, games, toys, clothes
- ▷ You almost automatically respond "No" to any decision she wants to make for herself
- ▷ You interrupt when she talks, you fend for her when she fights, you mop up when she spills the milk, you finish a task she begins.

How to Let Go

Before she visits, plan activities for yourself. Straighten out your files, put your tax records in order, or entertain friends. Tell her the specific times you will be busy, what you will be doing, and that you are not to be disturbed. Do not permit her (or yourself) to break the rule. Enforce it or you will be right back at the starting line.

Encourage her to select games and toys for herself, and to play alone. If this is too giant an initial step for her (or you), pick out a game, get her started, and let her carry on alone. Leave the room and work on a project of your own. Don't interfere when she's contentedly playing by herself.

Encourage her to invite friends for dinner, play, roller skating, the movies, or to spend the night, and to accept invitations to spend time with neighborhood friends or friends from her other home. Send her off lovingly, not grudgingly.

Let her learn to make her own decisions. Give her choices and let her pick. Ask if she would prefer to go to the park with a friend or just play outside. If she is unaccustomed to making choices, she may be intimidated at first. Don't overload her. As she becomes comfortable with decision making, offer additional choices. What type of clothes? What color? What would she like to eat? Which film would she like to see? Let her freely pursue the choices she makes, without interference.

If she stumbles after making a choice, wait before running to pick her up. Give her time to feel the result of her decision. If you respond like a dial-911 unit, you lead her to believe that someone will always be there to fix things for her, and you know that's not going to happen. Let her discover for herself that decision making is not a game, not a scary movie. It is real life, and sometimes has painful consequences.

Give her an allowance. It will start her handling her own money. More, it will give her a small area of independent decision making.

Let her solve her own problems. When she comes running to you to settle an argument with a friend, tell her that the two of them must work it out between themselves. Unless there are obvious signs of violence, don't get involved. Let her learn to fight her own battles.

Soon, sooner than you think, it will be time to let her go. When that time comes, — let her go, with love.

Chapter 17

A Letter to My Daughter

Dear Taryn,

When I think of the richness you have added to my life during the past six years, I recall a wooden chest of singular beauty that was a prized possession of my youth. It pleased me, naturally, when others found it interesting. But I was more intrigued than they, because I knew that concealed inside was a series of equally beautiful chests of gradually diminishing sizes. Others saw only the outer shell.

Throughout your life, many people will see only the surface of Taryn Hill. I will always see past the surface to the series of delightful personalities concealed inside, each evolving from the previous one, unified only by the spirit and the soul that express the essential Taryn Hill.

It has been my joy and my privilege to know you as a baby and as the strong-willed and independent girl you have become, and all those enchanting and ever-changing personalities between the baby and the girl.

I hold you, in my mind's eye, as I held you in my arms when, for the first time, I looked down at your dear and delicate face with awe in my heart, and said to myself, "My daughter. My daughter."

I see you at one year. One whole year, and my friends and I gathered in my apartment to celebrate your first birthday. We dimmed the lights and brought in your cake, pink and white and glowing as you yourself, reflections of its sparkling candles dancing in your eyes. Your little hand reached out toward, I thought, the cake, but it closed on a candle. Your screams lasted only seconds but they still exist, in memory, right alongside my agonized self-castigation for not realizing that a one year old would instinctively reach for the brightest light.

I see you, later that year, taking your first baby steps. I had knelt to hold you at arms length, encouraging you to come to me on your own, then I let go and you took a few steps, fell awkwardly against me, slid down, and plopped your well-padded bottom on the floor. You sat there and gazed up into my eyes, puzzlement and delight radiating in your face, just as impressed as I at your awesome achievement. Suddenly you squealed with glee, and both of us broke into laughter.

Soon you were three, and we made our first pilgrimage to Disneyland for the express purpose of seeing your then-hero Mickey Mouse. As we cut across Town Square, we came suddenly face to face with Mickey as he rounded a corner. Reality clashed with your dream and, for a few seconds, you stood still as a startled fawn. Then you ran the few yards to Mickey. He reached down and hugged you, and the happiness clearly evident in your face made me feel like a true miracle worker.

Soon your love and concern began to reach outward, beyond your familiar circle. One day at the zoo, as we crowded up to watch monkeys swing and swoop and crisscross from one trapeze bar to another, a particularly large and powerful monkey opted to swing, not to another bar, but straight through the air at us. His huge body slammed the cage, and the air vibrated with the sound of cannons. We quickly stepped back. The intervening wire could probably have withstood a hundred times the impact, but that fact in no way allayed our primordial fear.

I turned back to the monkeys and, realizing that you were not with me, I looked around to see you comforting a little boy who was sitting on the ground crying. He had wandered away from his mother and was standing by when the monkey struck. Frightened, he stumbled backwards and fell. You helped him up, and were reassuring him when his mother came over, thanked you, took his hand, and they walked away together.

About five minutes later, he was back again, standing by you holding your hand. Concerned that he may have wandered off again without his mother's notice, and wondering why she wasn't keeping better track of him, I scanned the crowd to see where she was. Our eyes met and I saw she was reading my mind. She grinned, shrugged her shoulders, threw her hands out, palms up, in an international parental language that plainly said, I know where he is. I'm watching him, but what can I do. I think he's in love.

Then you celebrated your fourth birthday. That was the year we knew moments of terror at Marine World Africa, USA. Remember the sprawling slide that dominated the carnival-like playland? The children would go up and once at the top, they could come down one of two slides, the first short and simple, the second covered, long and steep. Unlike most slides, the entire structure was covered over, so that once a child started up the stairs, she was hidden from sight until she emerged from one of the exits, which were at a considerable distance from each other, and anyone standing at either exit was unable to see the other.

You went up the ladder and, as we had agreed that you would come down the shorter slide, I walked around to meet you. (I later found out that, when you reached the top, the man in charge decided you were too young for either slide, and asked you to walk back down the stairs. There would have been no problem if the structure had not been covered; I would have seen you come down. But, as things were, once you were inside, I had nŏ way of seeing where you were.)

I waited for about five minutes, growing more anxious by the second, but you didn't come down. I forced myself to wait another minute, so you wouldn't be alarmed by my absence, my eyes aching from staring fixedly at the exit with the intensity of a cat watching a mouse. By then I realized something was wrong. And fear took over.

There must have been five hundred children playing in the area, but I was alone in an alien and threatening land, where every symbol of happiness mocked my terrorized mind and my frozen heart. I dashed from one group to another, beneath an afternoon sun that threw long rays aslant the playground, deepening and enlarging the encroaching shadows; through billowing merry-go-round music punctuated by childish chatter and squealing laughter; through air thick with flags and banners, and heavy with the scent of hamburgers; amid the swirling colors of rides and booths — desperately seeking you, or word of you.

The air turned colder, the shadows deepened, but no one had seen you. Driven by fear, fear of losing you, fear that you might be alone and dreadfully frightened without me, and fear of all the things that could happen to a child alone under these circumstances, I continued my frantic search.

Then a young boy told me he had seen a lady take a little girl, dressed as I had described you, to the lost and found area.

And indeed he was right. You stood just inside the door, looking out as if watching for me and appearing as lost and frightened as I felt. But without, my brave girl, a single tear. You ran into my arms and relief exploded into tears for both of us.

Next year you were five, and that was the year I visited your kindergarten. About halfway through the class, you raised your hand in response to a question the teacher had asked, and I heard you answer the question correctly, with composure and self-confidence. "Oh well," I thought smugly, "genes will tell." Then I tried to not grin too broadly, and to not look too proud. I finally brought my facial muscles under control, but it was as hard as subduing a bronco.

It was also the year you began experimenting with the power of the written word. You wrote (more precisely, you printed, in large, bold uneven letters, going up, down, and sideways) the first letter I ever received from you. A fine letter, crisp, clear, and to the point: "Daddy," it said, "I love you."

Thank you for these and for all the miracles, both happy and painful, you have created in my life.

Soon, Taryn, you will leave your protected world for that great exciting world beyond home and school, where you will assume responsibility for your own self-protection and self-discipline. Before that day comes, and it will come sooner than we think, there are some things I would like to say to you, so you will never have to wonder where I stand.

A word about the past. I was concerned, at first, about how you would respond to being a child of divorce, and I am grateful that it seems not to have affected you negatively, nor has it deprived you of love or limited your experience. You have received an abundance of love, which I believe is a child's birthright, from me and my family and from your mother and her family. Through your two families and their diversity of personalities and interests, you have been exposed to a wealth of knowledge and experience and adventure.

Now, about the future. I ask you to remember, especially in times of trouble, something I told you long ago: "When you hurt, Taryn, I hurt. Whenever you endure pain in any form, I will be at your side, in person or in spirit."

I hope you will always feel free to come and talk with me, at any time, on any subject, in any difficulty, in sorrow or in joy, or when you just feel like talking or playing a game of chess.

I will try to be completely honest with you, to tell you how I feel and what I think. I will endeavor to keep our communication accurate and open so that no misunderstandings will arise between us. I will do my best to avoid words like "must," "should," "should not," "ought," and "ought not."

I will frequently remind myself how it was for me when I was your age, at whatever age you are at that particular moment. I will listen to you, but I will not judge you. I will advise you, if you seek advice, but I will not solve your problems or make your decisions. The choices are yours. But I will be there for you in good times and bad. I will always be happy to see you.

I will never show you a limited world, but rather one of limitless possibilities, a world where women and men can, equally, achieve self-actualization and full development of their potential in the fields of their preference.

I will encourage your dreams, not my dreams. I will support your efforts to achieve autonomy, independence, and success, however you define them. I will always try to keep my word to you in these and all matters, and my sense of humor and adventure, and if I begin to take myself too seriously, I will rely on you to let me know.

My love for you will never be contingent upon your efforts, your achievements, your success, or your compliance with my ideas. You are not my daughter, the mathematician, or my daughter, the electrical engineer; you are my daughter. I will place no expectations on you. I will always love you unconditionally.

Taryn, you came into my life as a miracle, and you expanded my universe. I am indebted to you for great happiness, and I have tried to make partial repayment by creating miracles in your life.

You, Taryn, are the real miracle.

You make my heart happy.

Dad

September 28, 1988

Suggested Reading and Reference

Allport, Gordon W. *Pattern and Growth in Personality*. New York: Holt, Rinehart and Winston, 1961.

Alter, Judy. *Surviving Exercise*. Boston: Houghton Mifflin Co., 1983.

Arnold, Peter and Pendagast, Edward L. *Emergency Handbook*. Garden City, NJ: Doubleday and Company, Inc., 1980.

Bandura, Albert, and Walters, R. H. *Social Learning and Personality Development*. New York: Holt, Rinehart and Winston, 1963.

Bell, A. P. and Hall, G. Stanley. *The Personality of a Child Molester, An Analysis of Dreams*. Chicago: Aldine, 1971.

Bloomfield, Harold H. and Kory, Robert B. *Inner Joy*. New York: The Berkley Publishing Co., 1980.

Cooper, Kenneth. *The Aerobics Program for Total Well-Being*. New York: M. Evans and Company, Inc., 1982.

Davis, Adelle. *Let's Eat Right to Keep Fit*. New York: The New American Library, Inc., 1970.

Davis, Adelle. *Let's Have Healthy Children*. New York: The New American Library, Inc., 1981.

Doyle, Michael and Straus, David. *How to Make Meetings Work*. New York: Playboy Paperbacks, 1981.

Erikson, Erik. *Childhood and Society*. New York: Norton, 1963.

Hall, G. Stanley. *A Primer of Freudian Psychology*. New York: The New American Library, Inc., 1954.

Johnson, David W. *Reaching Out, Interpersonal Effectiveness and Self-Actualization*. Englewood Cliffs, NJ: Prentice-Hall, Inc., 1981.

Katz, Jane. *The W.E.T. Workout*. New York: Facts on File Publications, 1985.

Lakein, Alan. *How to Get Control of Your Time and Your Life*. New York: The New American Library, Inc., 1974.

Maltz, Maxwell. *Psycho-Cybernetics*. North Hollywood, CA: Wilshire Book Co., 1960.

Mindell, Earl. *Unsafe at Any Meal*. New York: Warner Books, 1987.

Meyers, Gail E. and Myers, Michele T. *The Dynamics of Human Communication*. New York: McGraw-Hill Book Company, 1980.

Piaget, Jean. *The Child's Conception of the World*. New York: Humanities Press, 1951.

Prince, Francine and Prince, Harold. *Feed Your Kids Bright*. New York: Simon and Schuster, 1987.

Robert, Henry M. *Robert's Rules of Order*. Glenview, IL: Scott Foresman and Co., 1970.

Samovar, Larry A. and Mills, Jack. *Oral Communication*. Dubuque, IA: Wm. C. Brown Company Publishers, 1972.

Sheehan, George. *Running and Being*. New York: Simon and Schuster, 1978.

Skinner, B. F. *Beyond Freedom and Dignity*. New York: Vintage Books, 1972.

Skinner, B. F. *Science and Human Behavior*. New York: Macmillan, 1953.

Smith, Lendon. *Diet Plan for Teenagers*. New York: McGraw-Hill Book Company, 1986.

Tegner, Bruce and McGrath, Alice. *The Survival Book*. New York: Bantam Books, 1983.

Yanker, Gary D. *The Complete Book of Exercisewalking*. Chicago: Contemporary Books, Inc., 1983.

Action Organizations

VOCAL (Victims of Child Abuse
 Laws)
P.O. Box 40460
St. Petersburg, FL 33743

Fathers for Equal Rights
P.O. Box 010847
Flagler Station
Miami, FL 33101

Child Abuse Listening
 Mediation (child welfare)
P.O. Box 718
Santa Barbara, CA 93102

National Congress for Men
210 Seventh St., S.E., Suite 12
Washington, DC 20003

Samaritans (suicide prevention)
500 Commonwealth Ave.
Kenmore Square
Boston, MA 02215

Divorce Anonymous
P.O. Box 5313
Chicago, IL 60680

Father's Rights of America
P.O. Box 7596
Van Nuys, CA 91409

National Council for Children's
 Rights
2001 O St., N.W.
Washington, DC 20036

PACE (Parents' and Children's
 Equality)
1816 Florida Ave.
Palm Harbor, FL 34683

Parents Sharing Custody
435 N. Bedford, Suite 310
Beverly Hills, CA 90210

Endnotes

Chapter 1

1.   Bloom, B. L., *Changing Patterns of Psychiatric Care*. (New York: Human Sciences Press, 1975).

2.   Bloom, B. L., S. J. Asher, S.W. White, Marital disruption as a stressor: A review and analysis. *Psychological Bulletin*, 1978, 85, pp. 867-94.

Chapter 2

1.   Frankl, Viktor E., *Man's Search For Meaning*. (New York: Simon & Schuster, 1984), p. 95.

2.   Dyer, Wayne W., *Pulling Your Own Strings*. (New York: A Funk & Wagnalls Book published by Thomas Y. Crowell Company, 1978), p. 23.

Chapter 3

1.   Wallerstein, Judith S., A summary of comments. In The County of San Mateo Family Court Services publication, *The Best Interests of The Child*.

Chapter 4

1.   Wallerstein, Judith S., Joan Berlin Kelly, *Surviving the Breakup*. (New York: Basic Books, Inc., 1980), p. 311.

2.   Hetherington, E. M., M. Cox, & R. Cox. *Effects of divorce on parents and children*. In M. E. Lamb (ed.), *Nontraditional families: Parenting and child development*. (Hillsdale, NJ: Erlbaum, 1982), p. 246.

3.   Wallerstein & Kelly, p. 219.

4.   Shinn, M., Father absence and children's cognitive development. *Psychological Bulletin*, 1978, 85, pp. 295-324.

5. Biller, H. B., and A. Davids, Parent-child relations, personality development, and psychopathology. In: A. Davids (ed.), Issues in *Abnormal Child Psychology*. (Belmont, CA: Brooks/Cole, 1973), p. 52.

6. Hess, R. D., and K. A. Camara, Post-divorce family relationships as mediating factors in the consequences of divorce for children. *The Journal of Social Issues*, 1979, 35, pp. 79-96.

7. Yates, Alayne, M.D., False allegations of sexual abuse, *The Psychiatric Times*, 1987, 9, p. 4.

8. Bresee, Patricia, Geoffrey B. Stearns, Bruce H. Bess, Leslie S. Packer, Allegations of child sexual abuse in child custody disputes, *American Journal of Orthopsychiatry*, 1986, 56, p. 562.

9. Yates, p. 2.

10. Interview with Arden Weinberg, J.D., San Mateo, CA, January, 1988.

11. Weinberg.

12. Bresee et al., p. 563.

13. Freud, Sigmund, A General Introduction to Psychoanalysis. (New York: Washington Square Press, Inc. 1965), pp. 345-6.

14. Freud, Sigmund, *Outline of Psychoanalysis*, trans. James Strachey, (New York: W.W. Norton & Company, 1963), pp. 27-8.

15. Yates, p. 4.

16. Yates, p. 2.

Chapter 11

1. Peterson, Jean Ross, *It Doesn't Grow on Trees*. (Crozet, VA: Betterway Publications, Inc., 1988), p. 33.

Index

A

Abuse,
  mental, 125
  physical, 126
Accidents, avoiding, 17-8
Activities,
  family, 113-19
  instructional, 115
  motivational, 115
Affection, 161-2
Allowances, 130
  appropriate amount of, 130
  duplicate, 130
Arbitration, binding, 47-8
Arbitrator, 46
Art gallery, 116
Art museums, 151
Association with child, 68
Audiotapes, 110
Autocratic parenting, 96, 97

B

Babysitter, 137-40
  how to find, 137-9
  instructions for, 139-40
Banks, Tazewell, M.D., 113
Bar association, 75
Behavior of former spouse, 65
Berne, Eric, 25
Bess, Bruce H., Ph.D., 62, 65
Best Interests of the Child, 48-55
  determining, 48-9
Biller, H. B., 39
Binding arbitration, 47-8
Bresee, Patricia, J.D., 62, 65

C

Camara, K. A., 39
Characteristics of child
  molesters, 64
Chattel Theory, 40

Child abuse statistics, 63
Child's room, 87-8
Child-centered time, 169-74
Chore Schedule, 129
Chores, 127-9
  age appropriate, 128
  assignment of, 127-8, 129
  complaints about, 129
  payment for, 127
Class size, 142
Communication, 14, 64, 99-111,
  161
  coding, 100
  computer, 111
  decoding, 101
  feedback, 101
  generating, 100
  receiving, 101
  responding to, 101
  sending, 100
  with school, 144-5
  with the child, 101-04
  with the family, 104-05
Compromise, 36
Computer communication, 111
Conference, parent, 149-50
Conferences, planning for, 36
Conferences with former spouse,
  36-7
Confidentiality, legal, 78
Confrontation, avoiding, 37
Cooley, Charles, 24
Counseling, professional, 16
Court decision, 48
Court mediator, 46, 47
Cox, M., 39
Cox, R., 39
Creditors, 29
Crisis symptoms, 16
Cultural lag, 144

Custodian,
  handicapped, 50
  mental health of, 50
  physical health of, 50
  stability of, 52
Custody, 39-70
  de facto, 43-4
  de jure, 43-4
  deciding, 45-6
  financial considerations for, 53-4
  forms of, 42-5
  history of, 40-2
  permanent, 43-4
  preference of child, 54
  psychological studies of, 39
  shared legal, 44
  shared physical, 45
  sole legal, 44
  sole physical, 45
  temporary, 43-4
Custody change, 55
Custody rights of father, 42

D

Dating, 153-8
  as threat to child, 154
Davids, A., 39
De facto custody, 43-4
De jure custody, 43-4
Default, 72-3
Development of child, 65-7
Discipline, 121-6, 165-6
  coordination of, 123
  lack of, 122
  physical, 126
Duplicate allowances, 130
Dyer, Wayne W., 25

E

Education, 52-3, 141-52
Electra Complex, 66
Eliot, George, 137
Environment, 27-8
Equal Rights for Fathers, 42
Exercise, 21-2

F

Family activities, 113-19
Family meeting, 104-08
  structure of, 107

Family practice lawyer, 74
Family unit, stability of, 52
Family unity, 116-17
Fathers for Equal Rights, 42
Financial considerations for
  custody, 53-4
Financial problems, 29, 36
Foods, 114
Frankl, Viktor E., 23
Free time, 159
Freud, Sigmund, 66-7

G

Games, 110
Games People Play, 25
Gifts, 110-11
Guidance of child, 52-3

H

Hammarskjold, Dag, 121
Handicapped custodian, 50
Hess, R. D., 39
Hetherington, E. M., 39
Hobbies, 117-18
Holidays, 88-9
Home environment, stability of,
  51-2
Homework, 148-9

I

Importance of father to child, 39-40
Individual play, 118
Indulgent parenting, 96-7
Insecurity, 159-60
Insomnia, 21
Instructional activities, 115
It Doesn't Grow on Trees, 127

J

Japanese Participative
  Management, 87
Job, maintaining, 29
Judge, 45-6

K

Kelly, Joan Berlin, 39

L

Lawyer, 30, 71-81
  changing, 79-80
  family practice, 74

Lawyer, cont.
  how to find, 74-6
  initial interview with, 76-7
  long-term, 74
  short-term, 73-4
Legal confidentiality, 78
Legal fees, saving, 80-1
Letter writing, 108
Letting go, 172-4
Libraries, 151
Looking Glass theory, 24

M

Manipulation, 131-6
  responding to, 134
Manipulation by former spouse,
  134-5
Manipulation of the child, 134,
  136
Mead, Margaret, 25
Mealtime, 114
Mediation services, 46-7
Mediator, court, 46, 47
Meeting, family, 104-08
  structure of, 107
Mental abuse, 125
Mental health of custodian, 50
Mental illness, 50-1
Moffitt, Philip, 83
Morality, 51
Motivational activities, 115
Moving, 83-4
  preparing child for, 84
Museums, 151

N

Negative reinforcement, 124
Non-directive Counseling, 170
Nutrition, 20, 114

O

Oedipus Complex, 66-7, 160
Operant Conditioning, Theory
  of, 124-5
Organization, 92-3
Organizing your priorities, 18

P

Packer, Leslie S., Ph.D., 62, 65
Parent conference, 149-50
Parenting,
  autocratic, 96, 97

Parenting, cont.
  indulgent, 96-7
  situational, 97, 98
Parenting partnership, 31-7
Parenting style, 95-8
Parks, 151
Permanent custody, 43-4
Peterson, Jean Ross, 127, 130
Petition, 72
Photographs, as method of
  communication, 109-10
Physical abuse, 126
Physical discipline, 126
Physical health, 20-2
Physical health of custodian, 50
  long-term, 28
Planning, short-term, 28
Plea bargaining, 68
Positive reinforcement, 124
Post-divorce trauma, 17
Principal, 146
Priorities, organization of, 18
Privacy, 88, 158
Professional counseling, 16
Prosser, William L., 71
Protecting against charges of
  child molestation, 61-5
Protecting the child, 70
Punishment, 121, 124, 129

R

Reagan, Michael, 85
Record keeping, 78-9
Reinforcement, 124
  negative, 124
  positive, 124
Religion, 53
Remarriage, 162-4
Report card, 150-1
Respect for child's mother, 35
Responsibility, 35
Responsibility for the child, 32
Richards, Bob, 95
Rogers, Carl R., 170

S

Safety, 118, 139
Safety of child, 50, 86
Sarcasm, 103
School, 141-51
  communication with, 144-5

School, cont.
    financial considerations, 142
    visiting, 143
    volunteering at, 148
School functions, attending, 148
School principal, 143
School secretary, 146
Security, 14
Self-help groups, 16
Self-image, 23-30, 170-2
    changing, 25-6
Sex, 164-5
Sexual abuse charge, responding
    to, 67-8
Sexual molestation of child, 56,
    60-5
Sexuality, Freud's theories of,
    66-7
Shared legal custody, 44
Shared physical custody, 45
Shinn, M., 39
Situational parenting, 97, 98
Skinner, B. F., 124-5
Sleep, 21
Sole legal custody, 44
Sole physical custody, 45
Special custodial conditions, 55
Sports, 117-18
Stability of custodian, 52
Stability of family unit, 52
Stability of home environment,
    51-2
Stearns, Geoffrey B., J.D., 62, 65
Stepmother and former spouse,
    conflicts between, 166-7
Stepmother, 163-9
    role of, 165
Stress, 17, 19, 84
Summons, 71-2
Supervision, 13
Support, 16

Surviving the Breakup, 39
Sutten, D., 169

T

Tantrums, 155-6
Teacher, 145-6
Telephoning your child, 109
Temporary custody, 43-4
Tender Years Doctrine, 40
Theory of Operant Conditioning,
    124-5
Toys, 118
    age appropriate, 119
Transfer of child for visitation,
    90
Trauma, post-divorce, 17

V

Videotapes, 110
Visitation, 39, 45
    deciding, 45-6
    preparing for, 91
    transfer of child for, 90
Visitation schedule, 88-92, 147

W

Wallerstein, Judith S., 31, 39
Wedding ceremony, children
    and, 163
Wedding trip, children on, 163
Weinberg, Arden K., 64
Welfare of the child, 13, 31
Women's movement, 42

Y

Yates, Alayne M., M.D., 62, 63,
    68, 69-70

Z

Zoo, 151